I0427673

# TABLE OF CONTENTS

# LIST OF FIGURES

# CHAPTER 1:  INTRODUCTION

## The Nature of the Problem

As the United States (U.S.) ends its wars in the Middle East and braces for an economic meltdown, national attention seems to be quickly shifting away from the Bush-era Global War on Terror (GWOT).[1]  With Washington's weakened appetite for foreign ventures, the United States has now withdrawn from Iraq and is planning to withdraw from Afghanistan in 2014, as directed by President Obama.[2]  Planned force reductions and massive planned spending cuts have U.S. planners contemplating force reductions and closing overseas bases.  As national leadership continues to struggle with dire fiscal realities, extracting a "peace dividend" by cutting national security might appear logical; unfortunately, unilaterally declaring victory in the Middle East, returning home and re-defining GWOT as Overseas Contingency Operations (OCO) fails to address the root causes that led to GWOT in the first place.  That is, radicalized Muslim Jihadists form an enduring threat to U.S. national interests at home and abroad, and those Jihadists seek to destroy the U.S. by all means possible.  Jihadists and their Global Islamist Movement[3] are the greatest security threat to the West[4] and to the United States.

---

[1] The phrase "war against terrorism" was first used by President Reagan in 1984 in reaction to the bombing of the Marine barracks in Beirut, Lebanon.  President Bush adopted the term in the days following the attacks of 11 September, 2001.  The phrase evolved into the Global War on Terrorism (GWOT) as a collective title for the collection of international campaigns and actions designed to oppose militant Islamists and al-Qaeda.  Although the Obama administration rejected GWOT in favor of Overseas Contingency Operations (OCO), the term GWOT remains in use by many political leaders, media and some official aspects of government including the DoD's GWOT Service Medal.  Many argue that the GWOT more accurately defines the purpose and enemy of the U.S. effort, and that OCO is so vague as to be useless.

[2] Lyndia L. Khalil, "U.S. Counter-Radicalization Strategy." *The Australian Strategic Policy Institute* 96 (January 11, 2012):  1-7.

[3] Islamist and Islamic must be distinguished and that distinction strictly maintained.  Islamic references a religion and a culture which has been in existence for over a thousand years.  Islamist references a political activist ideology which holds that Islam and Islamic law (Sharia) must guide all

## The Thesis

The United States must individually and collectively recognize the nature of the enduring threat posed by Islamist ideology and the Global Islamist Movement, adopt a Cold War mentality in the Long War,[5] and establish clear unifying statements of national policy designed to mitigate this enduring threat to U.S. national interests.

## Impact of the Problem/Thesis

The current void of clear U.S. national policy is resulting in discord among interagency leaders and between interagency initiatives. Further, when assessed against Islamist Grand Strategy, the void of targeted U.S. policy empowers the Global Islamist Movement and encourages the global recruiting of anti-Western terrorists. Although the U.S. Government is historically hesitant to enter into religious discussions, key aspects of Islamist ideology can be challenged in order to mitigate risk. U.S. counterterror strategies tend to address the prevention or mitigation of terrorist events and fail to address the motivating factors, which create the terrorists themselves. As long as violent and radical Islamist ideologies remain unchallenged, the United States will remain vulnerable to terrorist attacks at home and abroad.[6] Clear and public statements of U.S. policy not only serve to coordinate interagency action, but can also serve to inform global

---

aspects of human life: personal, political, economic, familial, and etc. Islamists seek the global imposition of Sharia as seen in Seventh Century Arabia during the life of Mohammad.

[4] Khalil, 1-7.

[5] The term "Long War" gained common use following the 8 September 2003 publication of an article by James Carafan titled *The Long War Against Terrorism*. In that article, the author discussed the enemy's staying power and questioned the possibility that the U.S. and/or Americans can ever be safe from Islamist terrorism again. As a result, the author advocated for a Cold War mentality to adapt U.S. will to successfully oppose our ideological enemies. To quote, ". . . we need to reaffirm our national commitment to defeating the long-term threat of global terrorism." The phrase and its concept were later adopted and popularized by Generals Petraeus, Abizaid, and others. http://www.heritage.org/research/commentary /2003/09/the-long-war-against-terrorism

[6] Khalil, 1-7.

public information campaigns designed to address Muslim misperceptions and to defuse grievances.

## The Analytical Plan

In order to derive specific policy recommendations, this paper will assess and discuss the politically incorrect[7] aspects of Islam upon which the Global Islamist Movement[8] bases its judgments and upon which Islamist grand strategy is founded. Only by defining Islamist doctrines, assessing their motivations, and recognizing their perceived grievances, can trends leading to the radicalization and recruiting processes be identified. After summarizing the established fundamentalist theory, which fuels the Global Islamist Movement and Islamist grand strategy, this paper then assesses published U.S. policy and strategy documents in order to identify their effectiveness in countering the Islamist strategy. The paper concludes by highlighting the gaps in published U.S. policies and offers recommendations designed to marginalize Islamists and mitigate the risk of anti-U.S. terror.

---

[7] Political correctness is defined as the use or avoidance of language, terms, subjects, policies, or behavior (as examples) which are seen as seeking to minimize the risk of offense. The term "politically incorrect" includes the use of language, ideas and behavior, which are unconstrained by perceived orthodoxy or by concern for the risk of offending or expressing bias regarding people groups. http://en.wikipedia.org/wiki/Politically_correct

[8] Counterterror strategists increasingly use the term Global Islamist Movement and this paper advocates for its continued use within the U.S. lexicon.

# CHAPTER 2: THE PSYCHOLOGY OF TERRORISM

Terrorism: Pre-meditated, politically motivated violence perpetrated against non-combatant targets by sub-national groups or clandestine agents, usually intended to influence an audience.[1]

– The Department of State

Following the shock and horror of a terror attack, it is commonly suggested that there must be something mentally wrong with terrorists who committed those acts of extreme violence against their seemingly innocent victims. They must be crazy, suicidal, or psychopathic. They must be devoid of moral feelings because only someone with something seriously wrong with them could conduct the horrific acts of cold-blooded murder that characterize terror attacks.[2] Thirty years ago, this was commonly presumed as true; however, decades of scientific study have now benefited from hundreds of study subjects, some of which were captured and now sit in prisons, some retired and returned home, and some successfully transitioned from insurgent movements into subsequent governments and now hold legitimate positions of power within those governments. Interviews with these terrorists rarely uncover any of the mental disorders acknowledged by the American Psychiatric Association in their Diagnostic and Statistical Manual of Mental Disorders. The presumption that terrorists are somehow mentally flawed has been thoroughly rejected by scientific study. As summarized in later chapters, individuals become terrorists in many ways and for many reasons. In the days following the attacks of 11 September, experts offered three common terrorist motivators: they were crazy; they were crazed by anti-United States (U.S.) hatred and anger; or, from their

---

[1] Chris Stout (ed.), *The Psychology of Terrorism: Volume III, Theoretical Understandings and Perspectives.* (Westport, CT: Praeger, 2002), 32.

[2] Ibid., 5.

perspective, their decisions were completely rational.[3] Terrorist motivations are not to be understood through the lens of pathology,[4] but rather terrorists emerge from normal psychology driven by a deep emotional commitment to their cause.

## Psychopathy in the Creation of Terrorists

There is no evidence to support a case that terrorists are psychopaths.[5] As one example, the mutual commitment, willingness for self-sacrifice, trust, and cross-group coordination, which were evidenced by the 11 September attackers, are all acts alien to psychopathic behavior. It is possible that terrorists might recruit and exploit an individual psychopath for a limited objective, but that mission would be a one-person, limited-scope operation, which required virtually no trust or coordination, and that mission would require a reasonable chance of success without suicide. Psychopaths are anti-social and cannot function in groups, while terrorists always operate in groups, either formal or informal.[6] Increasingly, the terrorist's psychological requirement of belonging is being satisfied by proxy over the Internet. Through the Internet, potential "Lone Wolf" attackers satisfy perceptions of belonging within a greater global community of like-minded believers.

---

[3] Stout, 5-7.

[4] Pathology; that is, mental illness. Psychological research confirms that terrorist are making lucid decisions based on their individual world view. Randy Borum, *Psychology of Terrorism.* (Tampa, FL: University of South Florida, 2004), 35-45.

[5] A psychopath is a person with a personality disorder characterized by shallow or void of emotions including a lack of empathy, cold heartedness, and lack of remorse. Stout, 6-9.

[6] Formal terrorist groups are designed and organized for an operation like a rifle squad; e.g., the 11 September attackers. Informal groups come together to form groups more spontaniously often through meeting associations at a mosque or Internet chat room where they come to perceive themselves as being a member of a group.

Anger:  Motivations of Insult and Frustration

The explanation that terrorism is a result of people blinded by anger is not consistent with what is known about the emotion of anger.[7]  Anger does cloud judgment and causes blindness to self-interests.  There are two primary theories related to anger.[8]  The first, derived from Aristotle, states that anger is the emotional reaction to insult or a perceived violation of respect or status.  The second theory states that anger is an animalistic reaction to pain, most commonly a pain of frustration where frustration is defined as the failure to achieve an expected or anticipated reward.  These two theories clearly share much in common; however, they differ in perspectives because insult is subjective while frustration is objective.  That is, insult is contained within the perceptions of the mind while frustration is the perception of being deprived of something.  There is no evidence to suggest that either motivated the 11 September attackers.[9]  As one example, and contrary to many media reports, survivor interviews suggest that Palestinian bombers were motivated rationally by the thousands of dollars of reward money to be paid to the families, not anger.  In the West, this seems to be a small sum of money, but within the crushing poverty of the West Bank, it is a significant incentive capable of lifting an entire family from abject poverty.  These are lucid acts of perceived self-sacrifice, not lunatics.

---

[7] Stout, 8.

[8] Bruce Bongar, Lisa Brown, Barry Beutler, and James Breckenridge (eds.), *Psychology of Terrorism.* (New York, NY:  Oxford University Press, 2007), 18.

[9] Stout, 8.

## Collective Insult and Frustration

Group identification makes sense of sacrifices by individuals who were not personally insulted or personally frustrated.[10] Indeed a vast number of post-World War II terrorists have been middle class with at least some advanced education, not members of a deprived population. Their perceived membership in a greater community provides terrorists with a sense of grievance against outsiders, which they internalized personally and which leads them to "defensive" counteraction. Historically, when Muslim populations are in conflict with their governments the West has supported those governments even when they are perceived as corrupt, unjust, or outside of the will of the people. This perception adds to the sense of anti-Western grievance and is highlighted in Sayeed Qutb's impactful writings.[11] The best insight into the motives of the 11 September attackers is a document found in the suitcases of many of those attackers.[12] The document does not contain lists of collective frustrations or insults. It contains no record of injustice or communal purpose. The sense of the document is that the attackers engaged in the operation solely to please God and to glorify the Quranic story of Mohammad's son-in-law, Ali ibn Talib, which recounts a battle wherein Ali was spat upon by an enemy infidel.[13] Ali is said to have held his sword until he could master the opportunity for revenge, "an individual and human motive," and acted only when he

---

[10] Stout, 9.

[11] Qutb wrote many impactful stories, books, and manuscripts including Milestones. The Jihad chapter in Milestones altered the course of political violence by calling for attacks against Western supporters and not the Arab governments which they seek to replace. Qutb's writings and followers were instrumental in informing Islmamist strategies.

[12] Bongar, et al, 34-37

[13] Infidel is simply defined as a non-believer, but the perspective of the judge is imperative. From an Islamist perspective, infidels are not only pagans, but they also include Christians, Jews (otherwise considered fellow "People of the Book") and other Muslims who are not activly practicing Islam in accordance to the expections of the Islamist.

could strike for God.  Rather than anger or hatred, the primary message of the text was eternal:  they were acting with God and for God against evil.  This resonates with long-established Western ideas of combat psychology, which suggest terrorists are more normal than commonly recognized.

## Psychologies of Cause and Comradeship

The developmental process through which normal people commit abnormal acts of violence requires time.[14]  Terrorists kill for the same reasons other groups have killed for centuries:  they kill for cause and for comrades.  That is, they kill for ideology and intense small group dynamics.  Unlike animals, humans are aware that they are going to die someday and, consequently, humans seek greater meaning in life and in death.[15] Religion, culture, values, and social norms are all powerful drivers in that search.  It is essential that "the cause" provide the promise of a long and glorious future.  History is important in supporting this promise.  A new cause has no history; therefore, it offers no long and glorious future.  An age-old cause has an age-old history, which offers a long and glorious future for those who serve that cause because they feel that they will be remembered.[16]

Like-minded terror groups define and focus group values with personal intensity.[17]  All humans belong to multiple sub-groups; examples include work, school, church, home, neighborhood, extended family, tribe, and clan.  The norms and values of each of these groups compete within the individual.  Members of terrorist groups tend to

---

[14] Stout, 12.

[15] Bongar, et al, 19-20.

[16] Stout, 11-12.

[17] Ibid., 12-14.

8

self-isolate so that the terrorist values displace other competing values. With this, individual balance is offset until those new radicalized norms and values drive personal conduct and judgment. This skewed and isolated view can make action against the enemy not only acceptable, but also required. Every modern army attempts the same process by isolating trainees, limiting their contact with their families, and removing their civilian clothes while they are indoctrinated into their new culture. Functionally, terrorist clusters, cells, and organizations do the same.

## The Psychology of Terrorist Strategy

Psychologists recognize two types of aggression: emotional and instrumental.[18] Emotional aggression is associated with anger, which, as mentioned previously, can often cloud judgment. Emotional anger seeks to cause damage and its reward is short-term, residing in the violent act itself. Many of the "green on blue" incidents in Afghanistan fit into this category and are not, by definition, terror attacks. They are shortsighted acts of anger-driven vengeance against some perceived insult. Instrumental aggression is more calculating. It is the use of violence as a means to a designated end. In analytical application, the two forms of aggression can easily manifest within the same organization where planners and leadership express instrumental aggression while foot troops express emotional aggression. Emotional aggression can inflict tactical damage while institutional aggression can force governments to expend vast resources in defense. A third psychological element of terrorist strategy can be the mobilization of the group to

---

[18] Stout, 16-18.

action.[19] Terrorists hope to inflict damage, which will elicit a disproportionately violent response thereby alienating the state and building the group's base of support.

## The Psychological Impacts of Globalization[20]

In most cultures, the globalization of world markets and world economies is generally considered as a good thing.[21] In the West, globalization is perceived as offering limitless opportunity for self-fulfillment, but that same globalization can trigger political and social instability. Globalization and Western capitalistic success both rely on an individualistic, impersonal, and privatized worldview. This worldview strongly contradicts the norms found in highly traditional and communitarian cultures, as is found in the Muslim world. In communitarian societies, individuals are linked through common interests, shared resources, and traditional mutual respect where intimacy and mutual support are valued and personal desires are subordinated to the needs of the group. In this clash, traditional social cohesion is weakened by the pursuit of material gain, personal freedom, consumerism, and mobility, and this turmoil can create a social-cultural identity crisis. As globalization continues to advance, traditional cultures, religions, and societies often view themselves as under attack by Western-led globalization. This is the beginning and major contributor to the creation of "the other" or an "us-versus-them" perception of outsiders. The creation of "the other" is an instrumental step toward the dehumanization, which allows the psychological dislocation required to commit horrific acts of violence upon innocent victims.

---

[19] Bongar, et al, 22-23.

[20] In this context, globalization includes advances in communications technologies, Internet and social media. It includes mass-global transportation and the external influences of Western democratic values upon the traditional societies under discussion.

[21] Stout, 37-45.

## Summary and Conclusions

The psychological study of terrorist organizations and of their individual terrorists is far from complete, yet over forty years of scientific psychological data has resulted in some decisive conclusions. Terrorists do not suffer from some form of mental illness or irrational rage as is commonly suggested.[22] Terrorists decide to act through a lucid and logical analytical process guided by their own worldview. Religion, history, and cultural norms play significant roles in their calculus and, as such, further study of those drivers is warranted. The impacts of globalization upon highly traditional cultures and the creation of a victim-mentality are proven motivators where anger results from perceived collective insult and individual frustration. Insult and frustration are linked because individuals see the ineffective nature of their own governments, societies, and economies as compared to the West. Political impotence in the face of largely thug regimes and the effective shifting of blame by those regimes toward the external, Western, "other" falsely indicts America as the primary scapegoat. As will be shown in detail later, the use of the Quranic narrative further justifies and rationalizes the external enemy paradigm, but within the context of a glorious Holy War. Here, the seeker's psychological need for cause and comradeship finds glorious stories of ancient Arabia with their romantic visions of conquest and modern rationalizations of violence as "defensive" counterattacks against foreign oppressors.

As will be shown, the focus of U.S. counterterrorism strategy has been placed upon those who have already transitioned into terror networks and are already committed to carry out terror attacks. This strategy fails to address the foundation where radicalization and recruitment begin. The basic issues at the foundational level need to

---

[22] Bongar, et al, 32-38.

be addressed by guiding principles including how the majority of Muslims perceive fairness, openness, and political voice within their own societies. Psychological study confirms that, at its essence, terrorism is a moral problem with psychological underpinnings. The challenge is preventing disaffected youth and other seekers from becoming engaged in the morality of terror organizations, yet history teaches that moral problems do not have technical solutions. As a result, the current terrorism problem is at odds with the current U.S. over-reliance on technology. Neither sophisticated technology nor increased military force can end terrorism in the long-term. Current U.S. polities to defeat terror are only short-term strategies driven by political needs rather than a scientific understanding of Islamist motive or strategy.

# CHAPTER 3: ISLAM AT ITS FOUNDATION

Know the enemy and know yourself; in a hundred battles, you will never be in peril.[1]

– Sun Tzu

Terrorism is but one tactic being used within the greater Jihad.[2] It is an asymmetric tactic, not a strategy. Indeed Jihad can be clearly traced back to Islam's prophet Mohammad, the Quran, and the historical texts which documented Mohammad's life, his rise to power, and his rule. It is impossible to understand Islamist terrorism without a detailed study of Arab culture, contextualized history, and Islamic theology.

## Perspectives on Religious Interpretation

Without regard to a specific faith, religious practitioners can choose to derive meaning from religious texts by one of three general approaches or worldviews: historical, allegorical, or literal.

- The historical view: deriving meaning within the historic context of the time in which the text was written where the text is perceived as a historic document with little literal impact on the present.

- The allegorical view: viewing the text as an allegory where the worshiper extrapolates meaning from those allegories so that the text is used to create parallels from the past to derive meaning for the present.

---

[1] Sun Tzu, *The Art of War, Samuel B. Griffith, translator.* (London, UK: Oxford University Press, 1963), 84.

[2] Jihad is Holy War and is not a "struggle" as is commonly attempted by apologists. It is a call to the community to respond by waging war against some defined enemy; usually an annual war of empirical expansion.

- The literal view: literalists view their texts literally; i.e., God wrote exactly what he intended and God's faithful are required by God to comply in the present.[3]

Westerners are often confused by overlapping and often interchangeable terminologies referencing Muslim populations within the greater conversation of Islamist terrorism. Salafist, Salafism, and Salafi are all forms of an Arabic word representing a puritan or puritanical form of Islam.[4] Modern Salafists originate from the Arabian Peninsula and predate the Kingdom of Saudi Arabia. Saudi Sunnis are Salafists, but are often referenced by the familial name of their religious ruling elite, the al-Wahhab tribe; therefore, they are referenced as Wahhabi. Both Wahhabis and Salafists believe in returning to the fundamentals of the faith, so both, by definition, are fundamentalists. Wahhabi, Salafi, and fundamentalist are synonymous terms, and this paper represents their views and objectives.

The concept of puritanical twenty first-century Muslims seeking to impose an idealized version of seventh-century Arabia upon humankind is important to the understanding of Islamist objectives. They use terrorism as one of the means toward the accomplishment of that end. Further, understanding the Islamist lexicon as it applies to

---

[3] Coyt Hargus, "Quranic Interpretation: True Messages vs. Manipulation," *International Affairs: The FAO Journal* XIV, no. 2 (February 2011): 20-23.

[4] The NYPD report defines "Salafi" as a "generic term, depicting Sunni revivalist school of thought that makes the pious ancestors of the early period of early Islam as exemplary models. As a result, Salafists seek to purge Islam of all outside influences, starting with the cultures and traditions of contemporary Muslim society and restore it to that of an imagined seventh-century utopia: the Caliphate. The Salafi interpretation of Islam seeks a "pure" society that applies the Quran literally, and adheres to the social practices of Islamic law (Sharia) that prevailed at the time of the prophet Mohammad in seventh-century Arabia." The report defines "Jihadi-Salafi" ideology as the "militant interpretation of the Salafi school of thought that identifies violent Jihad as the means to establish and revive the Caliphate. Militant Jihad is seen not as an option, but as a personal obligation, which is elevated above other moral standards." Mitchell Siber and Arvin Bhatt. *Radicalization in the West: The Homegrown Threat* (New York, NY: NYPD-IU, 2007), 5 & 86.

the threat is critical to the delicate work of targeting the threat among peaceful members of a religious population.[5]

Sources of Muslim Religious Meaning and Divine Direction

Muslims formally divine religious meaning from four sources with decreasing levels of significance: the Quran itself, the Hadith, religious commentaries and, lastly, local traditions.

- The Quran is viewed as the inerrant word of God as provided through revelation to the Muslim prophet Mohammad over a period of 28 years. The Quran (or the recitations) is a compilation of verses handed down from God to Mohammad via the Archangel Gabriel for the enlightenment of humanity. Muslims view Islam as the continuation of the Abrahamic traditions, but a correction to Judaism and Christianity. They believe that God required that correction because man, being inherently evil, had corrupted what started as good by departing from God's designated path. Therefore, God provided his word directly to Mohammad so that it could be documented and humanity could correct its actions accordingly. Only the overt "words of God" are recorded in the Quran

- The Hadith is a compilation of historic acts and stories from the life of Mohammad: what he said, what he did, and how he did it. They are the wise sayings of Mohammad, but are not attributed to God. Although Muslims view Mohammad "as only a man," they believe that he was a divinely-inspired man acting within God's will; therefore, Mohammad's words and deeds serve as

---

[5] A theory recommendation and a graphic which distinguishes these threat populations will follow in later chapters.

examples worthy of emulation. Further, the stories documented in the Hadith often provide situational context to the Godly revelations within Quranic scriptures. The Hadith are considered second only to the Quran as an authoritative source of Godly guidance.

- The commentaries of Muslim scholars vary slightly and begin to reflect sectarian divergence in Muslim theology. There are volumes of commentaries dating back to Mohammad's scribes and personal companions, and they continue to be produced today. The historic authors are greatly revered; therefore, the legitimacy of those famed works remains unquestioned by the various Muslim sects.[6] Based on concepts of judicial precedence, many questions of faith, law, and conduct are viewed as having been adjudicated long ago and are, therefore, firmly decided by law.

- Local traditions can fill voids not covered by other aspects of the authoritative texts above. The inclusion of local traditions provides for added diversity within Islamic law (or Sharia in Arabic), but only along the margins and only in the absence of other more authoritative divine guidance.[7]

Pre-Islamic Arabia: Mohammad's Environment

During the life of Mohammad, Mecca had become an important center of trade. Political and security issues in surrounding areas had altered trade routes and, as a result,

---

[6] Differences in the Muslim community, or Ummah, do exist. As summarized later within the historic review, Islam suffered a split shortly after the death of Mohammad resulting in the division between Sunni and Shiite communities. Sunnis represent between 80 and 90 percent of the global Muslim population. Sunnis can be further sub-categorized by the "school" or theological scholar they choose to follow; however, that analysis is well beyond the scope of this work. Salafist/Islamists are Sunnis and this work is strictly focuses on their perceptions, their theological interpretations and their worldview.

[7] Mohammad Amini, *Fundamentals of Ijtehad,* (Delhi, India: Aligarh Muslim University, 1986), 44-52.

the spice trade from Yemen, the silk trade from China, and others were all canalized

through Mecca on their way to northern markets and, ultimately, into Europe. As a

result, the power and wealth of Meccan tribes grew.[8] Mecca was also a center for

religious worship. The black cube (or Ka'aba) in Mecca had long been a focal point of

pagan worship and pagan tribes stored their familial idols inside the cube, removing them

only during their annual two-week pilgrimage to Mecca. As a result, Meccan

businessmen became protective of the pilgrimage and idol industries, and the annual

infusion of cash that resulted.[9]

The religious composition of the region is harder to judge. Anthropologists

generally agree that almost fifty percent of the regional population were pagan animists

of differing types. There was a collection of family and tribal pagan gods, as well as

object worship including the sun, moon, stars, rocks, and so forth. Christians and Jews

each represent perhaps twenty percent of the remaining population in the Arabia and both

are credited for assisting in the eventual formation of many of Mohammad's thoughts on

monotheism and some of his grievances against other orthodox monotheists of the time.

It is important to note that the Judeao-Christian monotheists present in Arabia during

Mohammad's life would not be recognizable by Christians today. Arabia was on the

fringes of Christian Byzantine control and Byzantine emperors had, by then, hosted a

series of conferences in Nicaea to compile and canonize the Christian Bible as an effort

toward the unification of Christendom. Prior to that effort, there were many sects within

greater Christianity which followed doctrines outside of Christian orthodoxy that were

---

[8] Coyt Hargus, "Ali and the Roots of Division within Islam," *International Affairs: The FAO Journal.* XIV, no. 1, (February, 2011): 20-24.

[9] Ibid., 22-23.

judged at Nicaea as heresy. Many of those heretic Christians converted to orthodoxy, but many fled Byzantine control and a portion of them populated Arabia. These "heretic Christians" informed Mohammad's view of monotheism and his later actions. Mohammad was born within this environment.[10]

## The Phases of Mohammad's Rule

Mohammad was born into a politically powerful tribe (the Quraysh) in the city of Mecca in 570 AD. At that time, Mecca was a powerful center of trade and a key transit point on the camel caravan routes between the spices of southern Arabia, the silk trades from the Far East, and consumers in Byzantine Europe.[11] Mohammad was an orphan, but was protected by powerful relatives and traveled with the caravans to the major cities of greater Syria. As his reputation of honesty spread, he was noticed by a wealthy widow. She proposed to him, and they married.

Mohammad was known to meditate alone in the nearby mountains and reflect upon God while sitting in caves. It was in one of those caves in 610 AD where the Archangel Gabriel first appeared to Mohammad, delivering a message from God.[12] In the beginning, Mohammad feared he was losing his mind and kept these strange appearances to himself, but he eventually confided to his wife. She convinced him that God was speaking to him and that he should listened to the angel. As revelations continued, he began to preach to an ever-expanding circle of family, friends, and tribesman. Initially, the greater population viewed Mohammad as a nuisance, but

---

[10] Roger Spencer, *The Politically Incorrect Guide to Islam (and the Crusades)*, (Washington, DC: Regency Publishing, Inc., 2005), 22-34.

[11] Hargus, "Ali and the Roots of Division within Islam," 20-24.

[12] Islamic City, *The Holy Quran.* Islamic City, *The Holy Quran.* http://islam.org/mosque/Quran.htm (accessed October 15, 2012).

eventually he was considered a threat to Mecca's status quo. Mohammad's call to his corrected form of monotheism and his demands that the pagans destroy their idols and convert to Islam came to pose a threat to Mecca's powerful elite; after all, the annual pilgrimage and its idol industry provided a consistent flow of religious tourists and their money into the city.[13] In 622 AD, Mecca's ruling elite decided to suppress Mohammad and his followers violently. Many fled, some were killed, and Mohammad fled with a small band of followers to Medina where they received refuge.

The early years of Mohammad's prophethood (610-622 AD) occurred in the city of Mecca and are characterized by a peaceful message of correction and conversion to this new form of monotheism.[14] As a result, the scriptures revealed during this prophetic phase appear to target the conversion of Christians and Jews into Mohammad's fold. The period and the scriptures received during those years are commonly known as the Meccan period.[15]

Mohammad's arrival in Medina marks the beginning of the Medinan period. In Medina, tradition tells us that Mohammad was well-received and was soon chosen to bring peace among competing factions, which he did. With his growing power, his following also grew. There was a series of armed conflicts, alliances, and broken alliances that included Christian and Jewish tribes of the area. Some converted to Islam and some were destroyed by the sword. It was here, during this Medinan period, where Mohammad was said to have received the "war verses." Over the course of several years Mohammad expanded his power base in Medina until, in 630 AD, he was able to

---

[13] Spencer, 34-38.

[14] Islamic City, *The Holy Quran*, 1-2.

[15] Spencer, 36-38.

counterattack Mecca itself and destroy his former enemies there. With the capture of Mecca, Mohammad's role evolved again toward the affairs of state. As the leader of a nascent nation, Mohammad acted as the all-powerful political and religious leader of all Muslims in an ever-expanding de facto kingdom until he died in 632 AD. Some scholars choose to end the Medina period with the attack on Mecca in 630 AD and define a third period of governance based in Mecca, from 630 until Mohammad's death in 632 AD,[16] as the Kingdom period because the Kingdom years are distinct from the years of war seen in the Medinan period. In the Kingdom years, the young kingdom had been formed and God's revelations to Mohammad shifted to topics of rule and governance. This fact makes that later period worthy of its own distinct analysis.

In summary, the Quran and the accompanying narratives that document Mohammad's life reflect the circumstances of their respective times. In the Meccan period, Mohammad was peacefully recruiting. In the Medinan period, Mohammad was a combatant leader. In the Kingdom period, Mohammad was a ruler administering a growing feudal kingdom. As will be shown, the conflict between the scriptures of peace, war, and rule creates friction among all subsequent generations of Muslims because of their long accepted concepts of interpretation, including abrogation. Muslim jurisprudence requires that more recent revelations supersede older revelations; therefore, if there is a conflict in Godly guidance, the war verses are more authoritative.[17]

---

[16] Islamic City, *The Holy Quran*, 1-2.

[17] Hargus, *Ali and the Roots of Division within Islam,* 20-24.

## The Caliphate: Mohammad's Successors

Jihadists revere the historic Muslim empires that once ruled vast regions of the world, including Spain. Arab revisionists seek the return of greatness denied them by the West and commonly advocate for the return of the Caliphate as God's ideal governance for mankind. What is "the Caliphate"? The Arabic title Caliph is derived from the word Khalifah that means successor or representative, with the inference that the person succeeded and represents the prophet Mohammad as the legitimate ruler of all Muslims and the Muslim kingdom that governs them; therefore, a Caliphate is a state led by a Caliph. The term Caliph evolved to assume increased significance with the Caliph as the authoritative ruler of the Muslim "Ummah," the global community of Muslims.[18]

The use of the term "Caliph" started immediately after Mohammad's death in 632 AD; it continued to be used over the centuries by the rulers of various empires that happen to have been Muslim. Those empires include the Umayyads, the Abbasids, the Fatimids, the Ottomans, and others.[19] The last Caliphate was positioned within the Ottoman Empire in Istanbul and under the leadership of the Ottoman Sultan. When the Ottomans lost World War I, rulers of the newly formed Turkey Republic wanted to create a modern and secular state following a Western model of governance with a Western-style constitution. In that process, Turkey's inherited authority to lead the Muslim world as Caliph (as the surviving remnant of the Ottoman Empire) was retained within its

---

[18] Hargus, *Ali and the Roots of Division within Islam,* 20-24.

[19] Spencer, 38-44.

modern constitution but allowed to go dormant.[20]  Officially, the last Caliphate was dissolved by the modern Turkish Republic on 3 March 1924.

Islamists view the centuries of Islamic imperial power as the ideal and worthy of emulation today.  They have deduced that the period of imperial power over the West failed because Muslims failed to keep God's commands and eventually lost God's favor; therefore, greatness can return only by Muslims returning to the ways of old.  Often, Islamists reference "the four rightly guided caliphs" (the first four successors of Mohammad) as the most ideal leaders.  They romanticize those early years because the nascent Muslim kingdom was led by men who personally knew and had relationships with their Prophet, Mohammad.[21]

### The Four Rightly Guided Caliphs (632-661 AD)

Islamists reference the earliest days of Islamic rule as an ideal worth emulation; however, historic facts are not always as romantic.  Historically speaking, questions of succession often seem to be tainted by power-hungry struggles for succession, frequently through violent competition for control of states.  A historic view of the "four rightly guided caliphs" is worthy study because it informs that which followed.[22]

Mohammad died in 632 AD with no surviving male heirs and without overtly designating a successor.[23]  In the strict and highly patrilineal society of Arabia, questions of succession caused immediate chaos within the young kingdom and resulted in the

---

[20] Theoretically, Turkish parliament possesses the constitutional authority to revive its status as Caliph, should it decided to do so.

[21] This under the presumption that proximity to the Prophet equates to God-inspired rule.

[22] Hargus, *Ali and the Roots of Division within Islam,* 20-24.

[23] Mohammad did have male children, but none survived childhood.  As a result, his only potential direct male heirs were sons-in-law through his surviving daughters.

polarization of supporters into two armed camps, each advocating for their own solution to the succession problem.[24] The first camp was comprised of those who supported rule by Mohammad's closest male family members, namely his son-in-law Ali ibu Talib and his family. In opposition, the second camp was comprised of those who supported the perceived wisdom of age under Abu Bakr, one of Mohammad's key companions. Historic perspectives[25] skew the various narratives, but the two primary candidates remain–Ali and Abu Bakr–and Ali is reported to have gracefully deferred to Abu Bakr in order to prevent discord within the community. Arab culture honors age and Abu Bakr was twice Ali's age, which likely greatly influenced the result: Ali was simply considered too young to lead the Ummah. In 634, Abu Bakr died suddenly and was succeeded by another relative, Umar. Ali sustained his confrontational opposition to the other Caliphs throughout.[26]

Umar ibn Khattab became the second Caliph on 23 August 634 and was assassinated on 6 November 644. His successor, Uthman ibn Affan, was confirmed by a council as the new Caliph and soon after was accused of trying to rule the Ummah as though he was a king. Uthman was also murdered by a disaffected follower in 656. Following Uthman's death, Mohammad's son-in-law Ali was selected to rule, but his selection as Caliph was not universally accepted. In 661, Ali was assassinated after

---

[24] The struggle throughout the years of the "four rightly guided caliphs" is controversial and open to interpretation based on Muslim perspective. This struggle results in the split between Sunni and Shiite Islam and the founding heroes of both communities compete for control of the kingdom. Many are murdered in the process. As a result, each of the two narratives attempts to undermine the legitimacy of the opposing narrative while reinforcing its own. A complete explanation of these years is well beyond the scope of this work and only a summary, generally accepted version is included here. Most relevantly, this version generally represents the Salafist population under study herein.

[25] The Shiite vs. Sunni naratives do not match completely because they each favor different heroes within this story. Ali is the primary hero figure within Shiite Islam; therefore, Shiite versions of this story glorify Ali's behavior and victim status. Hargus, *Ali and the Roots of Division within Islam,* 20-24.

[26] Ibid., 23-24.

23

ruling only five years. After Ali's death, the governor of Syria, one of Uthman's relatives, was able to overtake Ali's powerbase in Mecca and subsequently moved the Caliphate's center of government to Damascus thereby transforming it into a hereditary empire now known as the Umayyad Dynasty.[27]

The struggle between the two concepts of succession–qualification versus lineage–continued throughout the rule of the four rightly guided caliphs. The conflict came to a head in the series of battles that resulted in Ali's death. Many in Ali's family were killed, but survivors fled into Persia and evolved in a vacuum into Shi'ites or "Shi'ate Ali"–the partisans of Ali. The victors returned to rule Mecca and became orthodox Muslims or "Sunni"–"that which is common." With Ali's death, the now romanticized Rashidun[28] period of the four caliphs (632-661) was over. In the centuries that followed, the title of Caliph (the ruler of all Muslims) would simply move from capital to capital with the most powerful ruler of the day. Some led ruthlessly, some more benignly. Some used the Quran and Islamic scholars in order to justify their wars of expansion as holy Jihad. What is most clear is that a historic review of the Caliphates ("rightly guided" or not) proves that the restoration of caliphate rule over humanity offers little for modern aspiration. The primary stated objective of today's Islamists is the restoration of the Caliphate somewhere and then the expansion of that Caliphate to rule

---

[27] A key point to be learned by the series of murders, political intrigues, and infighting that occurred throughout the "four rightly guided caliphs" who benefited from direct familial relationships to Mohammad or were close personal friends of Mohammad is clear. Islamists have a revisionist historical view of this time of turmoil as though it was the time closest to the life of Mohammad and, therefore, is to be revered as the ideal. This Caliphate is often regarded as the model to which the modern world should revert in seeking God's will for humanity today.

[28] Rashidun is the plural form of an Arabic word/title for those respected people who knew Mohammad personally. They are perceived as being more spiritual and their accounts have increased authority. Milton Cowan, M. (Ed.), *Hans Wehr - A Dictionary of Modern Standard Written Arabic*. (Ithaca, NY: Spoken Language Services, Inc.,1993).

globally under Sharia law. Informed by the historic summary of caliphate rule above, Westerners can best understand the application of this Islamist objective by recalling Afghanistan under the Islamist Taliban.[29]

## Key Concepts in Quranic Interpretation

The designation of these three periods or sequential phases of Mohammad's early ministry become increasingly important during the process of gaining meaning from the Quran for two reasons: the use of abrogation to determine precedence between two seemingly conflicting verses and the manner in which the Quran was compiled.[30]

The concept of abrogation exists in many religions and exists within Islamic jurisprudence.[31] Simply put, when two verses compete, the newer verse overwrites the older verse–the newer abrogates the older. Muslim moderates might prefer to ignore this established methodology because the more peaceful scriptures resulting from the Meccan period all predate the violent directives from the Medinan period while the more recent Medinan period contains all of the "war verses" with instructions for Holy War or Jihad.[32] The arguments of Muslim moderates against the use of abrogation and against the war verses are of value within the Muslim community's internal dialog toward moderation, but they are outside the scope of this work which is focused solely on the foundations of terrorist interpretations. The fact remains that the Islamic concept of abrogation is a long-standing practice and is well-supported within the key and historic

---

[29] Hargus, *Ali and the Roots of Division within Islam,* 20-24.

[30] Hargus, *Quranic Interpretation: True Messages vs. Manipulation,* 20-23.

[31] Amini, 48-56.

[32] Hargus, *Quranic Interpretation: True Messages vs. Manipulation,* 20-23.

commentaries; therefore, the use of abrogation retains its critical value in the determination of Quranic meaning for Muslims today.[33]

The Quran was not compiled during Mohammad's lifetime.[34] Shortly after his death, and upon returning from battle, his successors noted that the people who knew Mohammad and had memorized much of his work were being killed. They recognized that the scriptures, sayings, and history would soon die off with them, so they commissioned a documentation effort that eventually led to the agreement and publication of the Quran and the Hadith, as we now know them. As the scriptures were assembled for potential entry into the Quran, there was a crosscheck process designed to validate proposed scriptures. Scriptures that were confirmed by multiple sources were approved and inserted. Scriptures, sayings, and stories that were not confirmed were documented, but were termed weak, or Da'eef.[35] The men who assembled the Quran could have chosen many sequencing methodologies, but they chose to place the scriptures in order by their word length, not chronologically.

It is easy to see the theological problem. Abrogation is long-established element of Islamic jurisprudence, but the sequencing of the compilation makes judgments of chronology difficult. Only by identifying which verses (or Surahs[36]) occurred within which periods can the reader find meaning; today's Jihadists find the guidance they seek within the War Verses and by the record of Mohammad's conduct of combat found

---

[33] Amini, 55-63.

[34] Abdullah Ali, *The Holy Quran – Text, Translation, and Commentary*, Damascus, Syria: Arab Press and Distribution, 1987), 12-24.

[35] Amini, 25.

[36] Surah is the Arabic word similar to the term "verse" which assists the reading in identifying and finding a partiular "verse" within the Quran. Cowan, *Arabic Dictionary*, 456.

within the Hadith.  Examples of the "war verses" which Jihadists view as taking precedence over earlier more peaceful verses include the following:[37]

> . . . slay them wherever ye find them, drive them out of the places whence they drove you out, for persecution is worse than slaughter . . . and fight them until fitnah[38] is no more, and religion is for Allah alone.
>
> (Surah 2:191)[39]

> . . . fight and slay them wherever you find them, and seize them, beleaguer them, and lie in wait for them in every stratagem of war . . .
>
> (Surah 9:5)[40]

> Fight in the cause of Allah . . .
>
> (Surah 2:244)

> Fighting is prescribed for you . . .
>
> (Surah 2:216)[41]

## Established Legal Precedence

Concepts of precedence are of primary importance in Quranic interpretation.  It is important to recall that deriving Quranic meaning is analogous to Western

---

[37] These select verses are examples of the 109 Quranic versions which call Muslims to wage war against nonbelievers for the sake of Islamic rule.  Some of those verses are graphic with commands to chop off heads and fingers, and to kill infidels wherever they may hide.  Muslims who do not join the fight are called "hypocrites" and are warned that Allah will send them to Hell if they do not join in the slaughter.  The following site lists those 109 war verses for reference. TheReligionofPeace.com, (2013). *What does the Quran say about violence.* Retrieved from http://www.thereligionofpeace.com/quran/023-violence.htm.

[38] Fitnah is the Arabic word generally defined as the time frame of persecution, rebellion, or strife.  The word is specific and references the Medinan period conflicts between Mohammad and his early Muslim followers and the existing tribes of Christians, Jews, and pagans which opposed his power.  Cowan, *Arabic Dictionary,* 888.

[39] The version of the Quran used here is produced in Saudi Arabia by Saudi Salafists and is readily available around the world and on the Internet.  It contains parenthetical insertions/clarification which moderate Muslims find unhelpful.  Those "clarifications" are interesting to the student because they display the Salafist interpretation and, because of their proliferation, are becoming increasingly commonly accepted, particularly in the West/U.S.  Surah 9 is the collection of verses known as the war verses.  Abdullay Yusuf Ali. *The Meaning of The Holy Qur'an:  New Edition with Revised Translation, Commentary and the Newly Complied Comprehensive Index.* (Beltsville, MD: Amana Publications, 2006), 233.

[40] Ali, *The Meaning of The Holy Qur'an,* 438.

[41] Ibid., 438-439.

jurisprudence.[42] In other words, there are cases in law that have been decided and are commonly agreed as resolved; therefore, reinvestigating or retrying those cases is counterproductive. The cases have been judged and the legal answers are known. In Islamic law, this same concept is foundational to everything that follows. There are founding documents and scholarly texts that previously assessed and judged many common issues. Similarly, many issues can be judged by analogy. As an example, if there is a historic case of destruction of private property (perhaps killing a neighbor's chickens), then the punishment and associated restitution can be used by analogy in a modern case where a neighbor's car causes damage. Attempting to change centuries of jurisprudence is very difficult and, as will be seen, can be very dangerous for the innovator leading change.

## Bid'ah: Heretical Innovation

The Arabic term Bid'ah is simplistically defined as innovation; however, the English word cannot convey the heavily negative nuance of the Arabic term.[43] To Muslims, innovation refers to some new idea, some earthly injection of meaning or doctrine to supersede that which God intended. It refers to any newly invented matter without precedent and in opposition to the Quran and its exegesis. Innovation is heresy and, within Islam, heresy requires cleansing by way of the summary death of the heretic. This concept is supported by Quranic scriptures and authoritative Hadith.

> He who innovates or gives protection to an innovator, there is a curse of Allah and that of his angels and that of the whole humanity upon him.
> – Mohammad[44]

---

[42] *Hargus, Quranic Interpretation: True Messages vs. Manipulatio,* 20-23.

[43] Cowan, *Arabic Dictionary of Modern Standard Written Arabic*, 678

[44] Mohammad as translated in Sahaih Muslim, Book 9: The Book of Divorce (Kitab Al-Talaq).

So whoever innovates in it [something new within religion] is as heresy, or commits a crime in it, or gives shelter to such an innovator, will incur the curse of Allah, his angels and all the people . . .

– Mohammad.[45]

Summarizing his study on the subject, noted and historic Muslim scholar Ibn Abbas said, "Indeed the most detestable of these to Allah are the innovators." As a result, any moderate Muslim attempting to reexamine the early texts, or a Muslim attempting to counter established traditional norms, is inhibited because their text criticism is viewed as unauthentic or as innovation. It is therefore heretical.

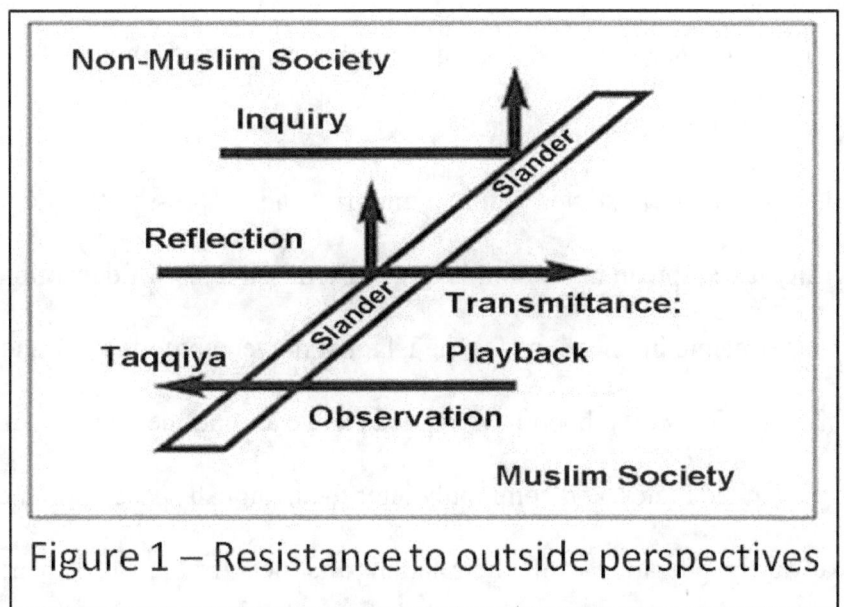

Figure 1 – Resistance to outside perspectives

[46]

As a result, and as the graphic above attempts to display, changing established traditions or the established Quran interpretations is virtually impossible, whether those established traditions are truly founded within in the Quran or not.

---

[45] Mohammad as translated in Sahai Bukhari, Book 80: Laws of Inheritance (Al-Faraa'id).

[46] Raymond Ibrahim, "Studying the Islamic Way of War: To know an enemy one must first acknowledge his existence," *The National Review*, Sept 11, 2008, from http://article.nationalreview.com/print/?q=NmE1ZTRmMDQxMDQ0ZmVmNWVkOTk5MmM5YTQ4NmFhZjg.

Taqiyya and Kit'man:  The Use of Deception

All of war is deceit.
– Mohammed[47]

There are two other concepts that modern terrorists including Osama bin Laden have cited as of great value:  Taqiyya and Kit'man.[48]  Both terms are found in the Quran and in the Hadith, and to most Western audiences the two Arabic words are so close in their meanings that only nuance separates them.  Both are founded in the Hadith (including Bukhari Vol. 3:857) and offer Quranic dispensation for Muslims to conceal their beliefs,[49] to alter the truth, or to conceal information by deceit in order to avoid "persecution" or to advance the faith.[50]  Osama bin Laden himself noted that value and divine permissibility of deceit within Jihad.

Although this concept started within a minority and suppressed Shi'ite population, during modernity it has spread into Sunni Islam.[51]  Permissible use of deception (or obfuscation) has strategic implications for the Islamist movement today.  Founding members of the Muslim Brotherhood have gained refuge around the world, including those within the United States, and commonly alter their English speech and their public commentary toward moderation while their actions and their Arabic words betray their

---

[47] Hadith Bukhari 4:267 and 269.

[48] Taqqiya is the permissive ability to lie to non-Muslims either to avoid persecution or to advance Islam.  Bukhari's Hadith vol.3:857 states:  "He who makes peace between the people by inventing good information or saying good things, is not a liar."  Retrieved from http://www.sacred-texts.com/ isl/bukhari/ bh3/bh3_ 856.htm.  Also, Cowan, *Arabic Dictionary, 332.*

[49] According to Ahmad ibn Naqib al Misri slander, or talebearing (namima),  is the requirement not to reveal things detrimental to Islam or Muslims. Al-Misri, Ahmad ibn Naqib. *Reliance of the Traveller: A Classic Manual of Islamic Sacred Law.*  Translated by Nuh Ha Mim Keller, (Beltsville, MD: Amana Publications, 1994).

[50] Al-Misri, Book R "Holding One's Tongue – Six Reasons Permitting Slander."

[51] Hargus, *Quranic Interpretation: True Messages vs. Manipulation,* 20-24.

Islamist intent. Westerners are hesitant to confront a clergyman and we presume that "men of God" are responding truthfully; however, Islamists increasingly use this divine authority to advance God's work by deception.[52] In a worldview where "the ends justify the means," skepticism is always warranted.

Takfir:  Branding as a Heretic[53]

In Arabic, the core word Kufr means a state of disbelief or a negation of faith;[54] therefore, a Kafir is one who is in a state of disbelief or who has negated his faith is Islam. That person remains in this state until his status is restored and, while in a state of non-believer, he has no protection under Islamic law. Linguistically, Takfir refers to the practice of one Muslim declaring another Muslim an unbeliever: the making of someone into a Kafir. It is rather similar to the Catholic concept of excommunication or expulsion from the Church. This judgment is usually the result of an act or statement that is judged as evidence that the person abandoned Islam. The use of Takfir[55] as a weapon, as a control mechanism, is not new and dates back to the rule of Abu Bakr, the first of the four rightly guided caliphs who succeeded Mohammad.[56] Islamist strategist al Suri touted the value of Takfir as a control mechanism to suppress opposition voices:

> For example, one tenet of Sharia Law is to punish those who criticize Islam and to silence speech considered blasphemous [defamatory] of its prophet, Mohammad. While the violent arm of the Islamist Movement attempts to silence free speech by murdering film directors . . . and by forcing thinkers .

---

[52] "A person should not speak of anything he notices about people besides that which benefits a Muslim to relate or prevents disobedience."  Al-Misri, Book R, "Holding One's Tough – Talebearing."

[53] Al-Misri, Book-O: "Justice – Apostasy from Islam."

[54] Cowan, *Arabic Dictionary, 888.*

[55] Similarly, the term Takfiri can be used to negatively reference those who advocate for Takfir. This format would be negative messaging to likely delegitimize an opponent's credibility with the public.

[56] Hargus, *Quranic Interpretation: True Messages vs. Manipulation*, 20-24.

. . into hiding out of fear for [their] life, the lawful arm is skillfully maneuvering within western court systems, hiring lawyers and suing to silence its critics.[57]

Because accusation of non-belief can come from anywhere, the threat of being branded as a Kafr through the use of Takfir is a real threat within Muslim societies. Moderate Muslims and Muslims attempting to counter the fundamentalist argument are threatened with Takfir as an effective means of silencing opposition[58] and reform.

---

[57] Brooke Goldstein and Aaron Meyer as quoted by Steve Emerson, "Combating Lawfare," *IPT News*, March 15. 2010, http://www.investigateproject.org/1858/combating-lawfare. 1-2.

[58] From Al Misri's Reliance of the Traveler per Islamic Law: 1) "The talebearer will not enter paradise." (2) "Do you know what slander is?" They answered, "Allah and His Messenger know best." He said, "It is to mention of your brother that which he would dislike." Someone asked, "What if he is as I say?" And he replied, "If he is as you say, you have slandered him, and if not, you have calumniated him." (3) "The Muslim is the brother of the Muslim. He does not betray him, lie to him, or hang back from coming to his aid. In fact, talebearing is not limited to that, but rather consists of revealing anything whose disclosure is resented, whether presented by the person who originally said it, the person to whom it is disclosed, or by a third person. The reality of talebearing lies in divulging a secret, in revealing something confidential whose disclosure is resented. A person should not speak of anything he notices about people besides that which benefits a Muslim to relate or prevents disobedience."

## Jihad[59] as Holy War[60]

Thus the Jihad may be regarded as Islam's instrument for carrying out its ultimate objective by turning all people into believers, if not in the Prophet-hood of Muhammad (as in the case of the Dhimmis[61]), at least in the belief of Allah. The Prophet Muhammad is reported to have declared, "some of my people will continue to fight victoriously for the sake of the truth until the last one of them will combat the anti-Christ." Until that moment is reached the Jihad, in one form or another, will remain as a permanent obligation upon the entire Muslim community. It follows that the existence of a dar al-harb[62] is ultimately outlawed under the Islamic judicial order; that the dar al-Islam[63] is permanently under Jihad obligation until the dar al-harb is reduced to non-existence; and that any community—accepting certain disabilities—must submit to Islamic rule and reside in the dar al-Islam or be bound as clients to the Muslim community. The universality of Islam, in its all-embracing creed, is imposed on the believers as a continuous process of warfare, psychological and political if not strictly military.[64]

– Majid Khadduri

## Conclusions: Islamists and Quranic Interpretation

As the graphic attempts to display, Islamist core values are centered on the Quran, its accompanying exegesis documents, and the established corpus of laws known collectively as Sharia. Islamist objectives are political because they view anything

---

[59] From the *'Umdat al-Salik*, Islamic law defines Jihad as "war against non-Muslims . . . signifying warfare to establish the religion." Koran Verse 9:5 states: *"But when the forbidden months are past, then fight and slay the pagans wherever ye find them, and beleaguer them, and lie in wait for them in every stratagem of war; but if they repent, and establish regular prayers and practice regular charity, then open the way for them."* Islamic law recognizes no authority except that which comes from Allah. In the Muslim view, Islam is not just a religion but a complete way of life governed by Islamic law that comes from Allah who is alone sovereign.

[60] Salim Malik. *The Quranic Concept of War*. (New Delhi, India: Himalayan Books, 1986), 60.

[61] Dhimmis are the Christians and Jews living under Muslim rule or within Muslim lands who must pay an annual tribute (head tax) to the Muslims in order to live in peace. They were (are to be) completely subjugated and many rules were passed in order to display their subjugation such as clothes, colors, and construction restrictions to list only a few.

[62] Dar-al-Harb, that portion of the world which is in a state of war. Literally, the House-of-War. This concept proports that all of the earth is either in a state of submission to Allah and, therefore, is in either a state of peace or a state of war.

[63] Dar-al-Islam, litterally the House-of-Submission to Allah's will; commonly mistranslated as a state or House-of-Peace.

[64] Majid Khadduri, *War and Peace in the Law of Islam*. (Baltimore: Johns Hopkins, 1955. Reprinted in Clark, NJ by Law Book Exchange, 2006), 64.

created by mankind as innovation and God's established rule (on a seventh-century

model) as superior to anything mankind could have evolved into since that time. Other

forms of government are unacceptable. Individuals who are not under Muslim political

control can live in "submission" by conforming to Muslim rules as subjects. Anything

outside of Muslim control resides within the "house of war" and is subject to Holy War

attacks in future inevitable expansions. Note the use of deception throughout the system.

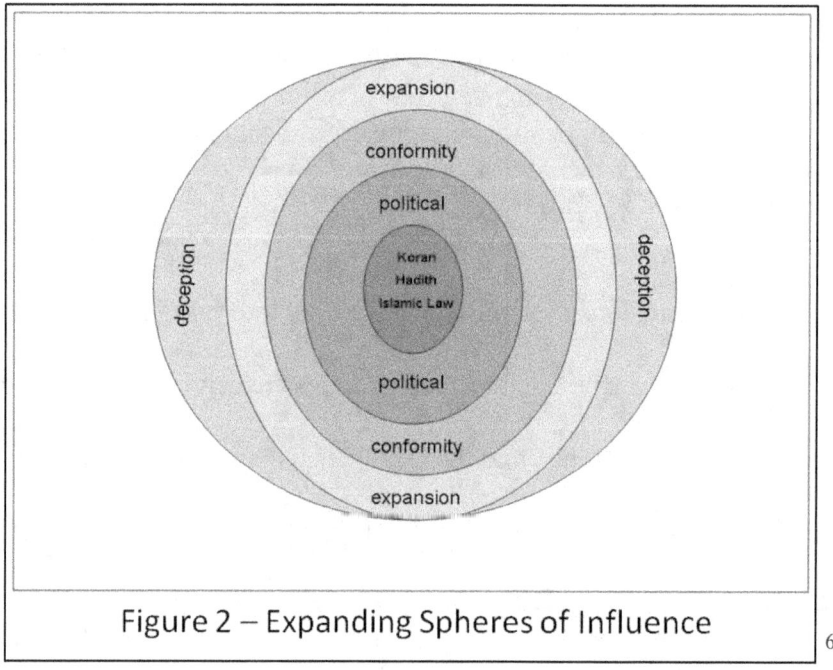

Figure 2 – Expanding Spheres of Influence

[65]

Apologists and Muslim moderates might prefer a different interpretive process,

but a study of Islamic texts and the authoritative process by which Muslims have

historically derived divine guidance reveals much to empower the fundamentalist Islamist

movement.[66] Although there are competing methodologies for interpretation, the fact

remains that the Islamist views are firmly based on accepted traditions, analytical texts,

---

[65] Raymond Ibrahim, "Studying the Islamic Way of War: To know an enemy one must first acknowledge his existence," *The National Review*, Sept 11, 2008, from http://article.nationalreview.com/print/?q=NmE1ZTRmMDQxMDQ0ZmVmNWVkOTk5MmM5YTQ4NmFhZjg.

[66] Hargus, *Quranic Interpretation: True Messages vs. Manipulation,* 20-23.

and established Muslim jurisprudence[67] As such, traditionalists, including Islamists, reject modernist Muslim arguments because they are invalid. Given the weight of tradition in the Muslim world, these facts have great weight and must be addressed, not rejected, by U.S. policy makers. Denying their existence does nothing toward addressing the threat.

---

[67] Amini, 86-94.

# CHAPTER 4:  THE CREATION OF A TERRORIST

> Some call this evil Islamic radicalism; others, military Jihadism; still
> others, Islamo-fascism.  Whatever it is called, this ideology is very
> different from the religion of Islam.
>
> – President George W. Bush

Globally, there are 1.5 billion Muslims[1] with multiple sub-divisions between

them, each with interpretive extremes on either end of the liberal-conservative spectrum.

Some might argue that all Muslims are bad, while others counter, "Islam is a religion of

peace."  Accepting diversity within the population, painting Islam exclusively as a

religion of peace, ignores the reality that militant Islamists and historic Muslim figures

have exploited Islam, through misuse of religious impulses, to induce individuals to take

direct violent action against Muslims and non-Muslims alike.  It is in the United States'

(U.S.) national interests to understand and successfully isolate Islamist ideology from

Islam/Muslims, mitigate Islamist influence by delegitimizing them, and negate Islamist

recruiting tools by engaging in the war of ideas that fuels their membership.[2]

Islamist:  A Precise Definition of the Threat Population

Islamists are individuals calling for Islam as a political as well as a religious

system.  Primary Islamist objectives include the forced implementation of Sharia law as

the basis of government and societal law as conducted by the earliest adherents of Islam

in seventh-century Arabia.  Islamists also assert that Sharia requires the elimination of all

non-Islamic influences in the political, economic, social, and, military aspects of human

life.  According to Youssef Aboul-Enein, Islamism is the idea of initially reestablishing

---

[1] Youssef Aboul-Enein, *Militant Islamist Ideology:  Understanding the Global Threat*, (Annapolis, MD:  Naval Institute Press, 2010), 2.

[2] Ibid., 7-8.

the Caliphate anywhere possible and subsequently expanding Islamist control to recapture the former "Muslim Lands" with the ultimate goal of global submission to God's rule (under Sharia) globally. An Islamist is, therefore, one who believes in that ideal. A Jihadist is one who believes in that ideal and is willing to use violence, kill, and even kill himself in order to achieve those Islamist ideals. Islamists call for a strict interpretation of the Quran, as the record of divine revelation, and the Hadith, as the record of Mohammad's acts and deeds. Their narrow interpretation opposes the beliefs of moderate Muslims and non-Muslims. Islamists oppose Western democracies and modern forms of government within the Muslim world as human creations outside the will of God. Militant Islamists (such as al-Qaeda and their growing list of franchises) also oppose the Islamist political parties (such as the Muslim Brotherhood) which attempt to advance Islamist agenda by participating in the political process which they intend to replace.[3]

Islamists can be grouped into three general categories based upon the individual action-mechanism they use to bring these Islamist views into being: individual, political, and militant. Individual (or "practical") Salafists (also known as Salafi Illmi in Arabic) are individuals who hope to attain the Islamist state through Dawa, or personal proselytizing. They do not see value in participating in corrupt regimes through the political process and are not willing to assume a violent posture. They feel that grassroots changes in neighborhoods and society will lead to the success of their eventual goal: the reestablishment of a fundamentalist Islamist state. They advance toward their

---

[3] Aboul-Enein, 2-4.

37

objective by funding mosques and schools, and through evangelism.[4]  As seen over

recent decades, these charities and schools have been used to support or divert critical

support to violent ends.  As will be shown, the Muslim data available to the seeker is

almost exclusively Salafist, which is directly related to this effort to "evangelize" the

world.  Political Islam has become a common-use term and accurately references those

Islamists who choose the ballot box and political parties as their desired means to the

same Islamist end state.[5]  As recently seen, within the context of the Arab Spring

uprisings, political Islamists (like Turkey's ruling Justice and Development Party, AKP)

are increasingly successful in assuming power from the chaos of "democratic

revolutions."[6]  The term militant Islamist refers to groups and individuals advocating

Islamist ideological goals, principally by violent means.  Al-Qaeda is only one militant

Islamist group, but it has morphed into a global franchise organization–a seemingly

growing family of like-minded Violent Extremist Organizations (or VEOs).

Aboul-Enein's theory attempts to put structure to his observations of the Ummah and

militant Islamists within the Ummah.  Islamists and Salafists are synonyms for Sunni

Wahabbis, as introduced earlier, but in his model Wahhabi Salafists are assessed as a

subset of the Maliki school.  (See Figure 3.)  In his book, *Militant Islamist Ideology:*

*Understanding the Global Threat,* Aboul-Enein[7] advocated that the United States should

---

[4] Aboul-Enein, 8-9.

[5] Ibid., 5-6.

[6] Peter Beaumont and Patrick Kingsley, "Violent Tide of Salafism Threatens the Arab Spring," *The Guardian,* http://www.guardian.co.uk/world/2013/feb/09/violent-salafists-threaten-arab-spring-democracies. (accessed February 9, 2013).

[7] Youssef Aboul-Enein has written three noteworthy books and several journal articles to date.  As a moderate American Muslim his informed and authoritative voice add greatly to the internal Muslim community conversation.  The referenced work on Islamists and his book on Iraq are must reads for anyone working related U.S. policy issues.

only target the militant population and, in doing so, attempt to co-opt the other Salafist

populations to inform on the Salafist militants (per Figure 4).[8]

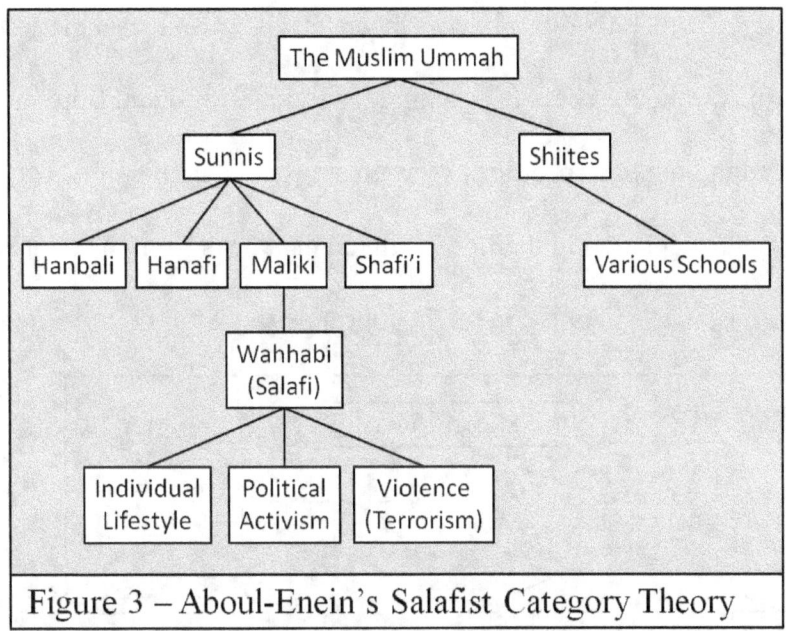

Figure 3 – Aboul-Enein's Salafist Category Theory

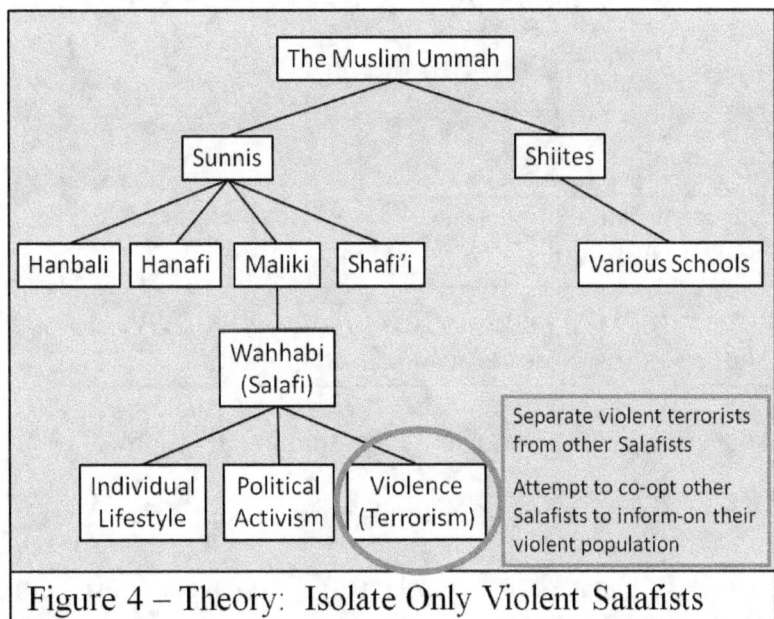

Figure 4 – Theory:  Isolate Only Violent Salafists

This theory fails to recognize that Islamists progress toward Islamism without

regard to sectarian origins.  Further, Islamists hold the same core ideology and seek the

same ideological end states without regard to sectarian origin.  Those Islamist objectives

[8] Aboul-Enein, 22-31.

are counter to long-term U.S. ideology and U.S. interests, but targeting only militants addresses only the near-term threat. As will be seen later, research published by the New York Police Department's (NYPD) Intelligence Unit (IU) provides a model for the progressive radicalization process of "seeking" individuals sourced from the greater Muslim population,[9] not one specific sub-group as Aboul-Enein's model suggests. A more likely graphic depiction of the flow of fundamentalists from the entire Sunni Ummah into the Islamists population might appear as shown in Figure 5 below:

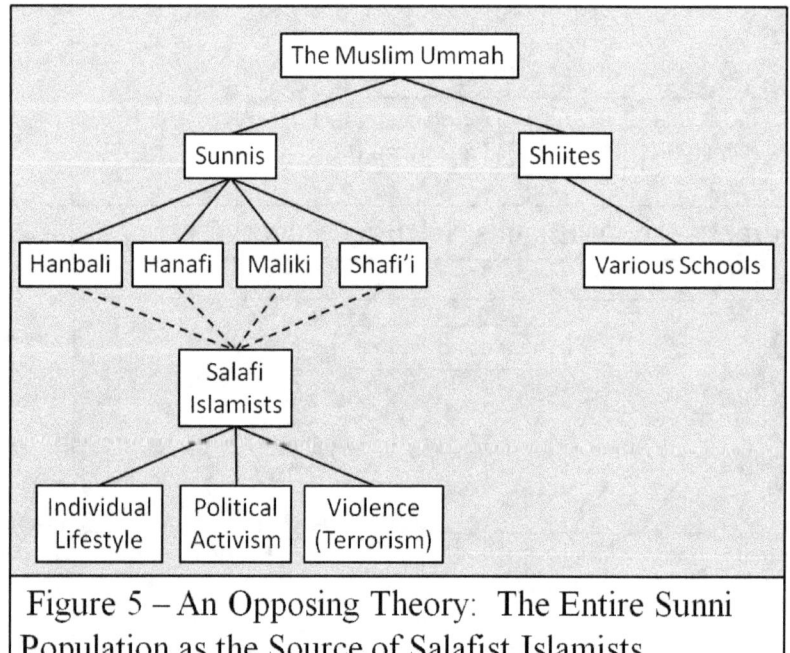

Figure 5 – An Opposing Theory: The Entire Sunni Population as the Source of Salafist Islamists

Within the greater conversation of delegitimizing the Islamist agenda, specific terms possess power and the use of those terms must be deliberate. The term "Jihadist" is viewed by militants as a badge of honor. Islamists must be distinguished from Islam and Muslims. Although their desired end states are identical, political Islamists are less of a near-term threat to Western interests than are the violent militants. Some scholars, including Aboul-Enein, opine that only the militant Islamists are U.S. adversaries and

---

[9] Silber and Bhatt, 2-22.

that the United States should attempt to exploit fissures between the militants and the other Salafists; however, Aboul-Enein acknowledges that all Salafists desire the establishment of an Islamic state which would ultimately "bare animosity" toward the United States.[10] As a result, and at some level, all Salafist individuals, organizations, and states seek ideological objectives which are directly opposed to American ideology[11] and modern Western liberal democratic societies. U.S. leadership must recognize this fact and openly state it within national security documents. It could be argued that the United States should carefully measure its cooperation with and support to any Salafist state that, by definition, seeks U.S. destruction. "The risks of not engaging in the ideological conflict are too high to ignore because this enemy places much emphasis on the war of perception."[12]

## The Progressive Path toward Radicalization

> Violent Islamist ideology and the terrorism it inspires is a substantial threat to the security, Americans, and U.S. national interests. The core tenets of this violent ideology are straightforward, uncompromising, and absolute. The ideology calls for the pursuit and creation of a global Islamist state–*a Caliphate*–that unites all Muslims–*their Ummah*–and is governed by Islamic law–*Sharia*. In pursuing this totalitarian goal, violent Islamists are not only encouraged to attack those who are not committed to their ideology in its purest form, including other Muslims, but are purportedly obligated to do so.[13]
>
> – Dr. Marc Sageman

---

[10] Aboul-Enein, 20-44.

[11] As delineated in the U.S. Declaration of Independence (4 July 1776) and the U.S. Constitution (17 September 1787).

[12] Aboul-Enein, 20-58

[13] Noting the testimony of the author/scholar Dr. Marc Sageman, the Senate Report included this quote from Sageman's spoken testimony which, although responding to domestic terror questions, the same concepts apply generally across the global Ummah. U.S. Senate Committee on Homeland Security and Governmental Affairs. (Senator Joseph Lieberman, Chairman). *Violent Islamist Extremism, the Internet and the Homegrown Terrorist Threat.* May, 2008. 2.

Variant models explaining the progression and development of terrorists through the radicalization process exist. Although each model is unique in some manner, all of the various models are strikingly similar. Among those competing models, researchers from the NYPD's IU produced one of the earliest and most renowned. The IU's findings were summarized and published in 2007 within its impactful report, *Radicalization in the West: The Homegrown Threat*.[14] Although that report focuses on domestic terrorism, its findings are universal and have application across the field toward understanding, identifying and potentially intercepting the escalating radicalization process of Islamist terrorists, domestic and international.

Terrorists are not created overnight; therefore, the best way to combat the threat posed by terrorism is to understand better the process through which the means the terrorists are created. The process through which seeking individuals become violent Islamist extremists starts with the "spark" of enlistment. It is this message which the leaders of the Global Islamist Movement use to attract new followers.[15] The "spark" message contains three elements: (1) led by the United States, the West is engaged in war against Islam; (2) Muslims have theological justification and are obligated to defend Islam and the greater Muslim community; and (3) violence is required.[16] The radicalization process attracts recruits from the entire Muslim population. Although diverse sects exist within the greater Sunni Muslim population, no one sectarian population sources violent terrorism. Instead, seeking individuals progress from religious worship into conservatism, which may progress to fundamentalism, which may progress

---

[14] Silber and Bhatt, 2-28

[15] U.S. Senate, 4-5.

[16] Silber and Bhatt, 2-24.

to militantism, which may advance to violent "acts of defensive war" commonly mislabeled in the West as terrorism.[17] The NYPD-IU breaks the process into four distinct phases with marked characteristics for each phase.

## Phase I: Pre-Radicalization

The pre-radicalization phase is defined as the point of origin, perspective, or pre-conditioning of an individual before entering the radicalization process.[18] The seeker's worldview greatly influences the individual's progress through the radicalization process. Individuals who have been repeatedly exposed to propaganda themes are increasingly likely to assume a perspective of perceived grievance and to direct frustration toward their perceived attacker.[19] This person is the "seeker," often searching to fill some missing element from within his or her own lives. This seeker forms the fodder from which terrorists develop.[20] These individuals come from the general Muslim population; therefore, localized culture plays an important role in the normalization of radical or anti-Western attitudes. The more those perceptions of grievance and attitudes of frustration are normalized within a given community, then the more likely it is that the community will produce Islamists and, therefore, terrorists. This is an individual process resulting in individual, like-minded recruits. These seeking recruits are more likely to act when they are able to cluster into mutually supportive clusters, but they are fully capable of acting as individuals.[21]

---

[17] Bongar, et al, 56-84.

[18] Silber and Bhatt, 20-32.

[19] Bongar, et al, 34-46

[20] Borum, 4-12.

[21] Marc Sageman. *Leaderless Jihad: Understanding Terrorist Networks in the Twenty-First Century*. (Philadelphia, PA: University of Pennsylvania Press, 2008), 50-76.

Of note to the homegrown terrorist threat, in 2011, Pew Research reported the

results of a research project titled *Muslim Americans: Middle Class and Mostly*

*Mainstream* that concluded American Muslims[22] are largely assimilated into society and

are generally happy. Alarmingly, the report cited that five percent of respondents had a

favorable opinion of al-Qaeda.[23] The report found that eight percent of American

Muslims[24] find suicide bombings against civilian targets are "often" (one percent) or

"sometimes" (seven percent) an acceptable tactic and stated that 27 percent declined to

respond. [25] These numbers imply that up to 35 percent of American Muslims support

terrorist tactics, an alarming indication of the successful normalization of militant

Islamist precepts within this comparatively moderate population. This fact has

implications for national security and defense policy.[26]

Phase II: Self-Identification

Seeking individuals are influenced by others, the Internet, or both as they begin to

explore Salafism. In this phase, they gradually evolve away from their old identity and

---

[22] The 2010 U.S. Regional Census data showed Islam as the fastest growing religion in the U.S. over the past 10 years with 2.6 million Muslims living within the U.S., an increase of one million since 2000. Neal, M., (2012). "Number of Muslims in the U.S. Doubles Since 9/11." The Daily News. Retrieved from http://www.nydailynews.com/news/national/number-muslims-u-s-doubles-9-11-article-1.1071895.

[23] That percentage, if representative of the population, indicates that 702,000 American Muslims refused to respond to the question and, therefore, declined an opportunity to condem the suicide bombing of civilian targets which begs question: why not? This seems to indicate the population size of Salafist support to Jihadists tactics discussed herein.

[24] That percentage implies that 208,000 American Muslims support suicide bombing against civilian victims. It appears noteworthy that this population was "bold" enough to openly support terrorism.

[25] Pew Research. *Muslim Americans: Middle Class and Mostly Mainstream.* (2011) http://www.pewresearch.org /2007/05/22/muslim-americans-middle-class-and-mostly-mainstream/

[26] Estimating the American Muslim population within the Department of Defense is difficult, but the gross population is estimated to be around 15,000. Yazi Dreazen, "Muslim Population in the Military Raises Difficult Issues." *The Wall Street Journal*, (2009), http://online.wsj.com/article/ SB125755 853525 335343.html (accessed February 15, 2013).

begin to self-identify with like-minded individuals and adopt the Islamist ideology as their own.[27] In this phase, these seeking individuals evolve completely from their old, often secular, identities into far more fundamentalist forms of themselves. They begin to take on the outward trappings of faith to include traditional "Islamic" dress, food, and music in ways that previously did not interest them. Females, as an example, may begin wearing traditional coverings that they did not grow up wearing. These early recruits increasingly comply with the traditional aspects of Muslim worship and become increasingly confrontational with other Muslims who are not "Muslim enough" from their new worldview.[28] Because of their new aggressiveness, these increasingly conservative recruits isolate themselves from moderates–even their own family members–and that loss or rejection of a moderating voice further fuels the radicalization process.[29]

Phase III: Indoctrination

In this phase individuals progressively intensify their fundamentalist religious beliefs, including the complete adoption of the Salafist-Jihadi ideology with its global Islamist political objectives. This phase is marked by the acceptance of the idea that the condition and circumstances exist where their personal action is required to support, defend, and advance the Islamist cause. While individual self-identification may be a personal process, the association with like-minded Islamists is an important factor as individuals progress deeper into the terrorist-development process.[30] Where the

---

[27] Silber and Bhatt, 12-32.

[28] Borum, 78-84.

[29] Sageman, 38-52

[30] Silber and Bhatt, 32-44.

formation of interpersonal cells was once required for would-be terrorists to progress

further, the psychological function of those personal connections is now often satisfied on

the Internet in chat rooms and in email conversations with facilitators like Anwar al-

Awlaki.[31]  In recent years, the Internet replaced the requirement for personal mentors, the

requirement for a legitimizing religious facilitator, and the collective validation of a

group, thus leading to the concept of "leaderless Jihad" proposed by Marc Sageman[32] and

demonstrated by Major Nidal Malik Hasan, "the Fort Hood shooter."[33]

Phase IV:  Jihadization

During this final stage, recruits, developing as individuals or as members of a

cluster, come to accept their individual responsibilities and duties to participate in violent

terrorist activity as a justifiable means to a noble end.  Thus, it becomes a moment of

individual decision.  Although self-designated, they view themselves as holy warriors,

Jihadists, or Mujahedeen, defending the Muslim faith as warriors have done since

Mohammad's time.  In this stage, they begin operational planning toward a terrorist

attack where these "acts in the furtherance of" include efforts to plan, research,

---

[31] Anwar al-Awlaki was the American born Jihadist who became known as a talented recruiting and motivator of a Western Jihadists via the Internet.  He was involved in planning terror operations for al-Qaeda and was linked to the 9/11 hijackers, Army Major Nidal Malik Hasan, the "shoe bomber," the "underwear bomber," and others.  He was killed in 2011 in a U.S. drone strike.  Jarret Brachman and Alix Lavine.  *"You Too Can Be Awlaki!"  The Fletcher Forum of World Affairs Journal* 35, no. 25 (Winter, 2001).  25-46.

[32] Sageman, 84-86.

[33] U.S. Army Major Nidal Malik Hasan stands accused of murdering 13 and injuring over 30 during his shooting spree at Fort Hood on 5 November 2009.  He has become known as the "Fort Hood shooter."  Hasan's court-martial has not yet taken place, but reporting indicates that his radicalization process was taking place openly over many years.  His colleagues and superiors expressed "deep concerns" about his inappropriate behavior yet his path through radicalization to active-shooter was not intercepted.  Borum, 76-84.

reconnaissance, train, acquire material, and execute an attack.[34] Research confirms that, in recent years, most of the research and training required by Western homegrown terrorists is conducted on the Internet. "Lone wolf" actors like Major Hassan are a relatively new development that likely foretells the future of Islamist terrorist attacks within the West. As noted, Islamist Internet sites, strategy, and data have evolved to encourage this new tactic and these "lone wolves" require no physical group, or group affiliation.[35] Their very anonymity adds to their lethality, and the shock of a U.S. Army major murdering his colleagues adds the psychological impact that, by definition, terrorism requires.[36]

## The Radicalization Funnel

In summary, the NYPD-IU's analysis and its phased definitions of the radicalization process can be viewed as a funnel (see Figure 6) where a given population forms the Phase I environment and is the source of potential recruits. As one individual enters the funnel they might continue to progress through the phases, while others might not. While there might be a limited number of attackers who depart the bottom of the funnel by executing an attack, it is important to note that there are like-minded supporters still in the latter stages of the funnel. Not all Jihadists become attackers—as introduced earlier, there are other acceptable forms of Jihad that are equally critical to the support of violent Jihad.[37]

---

[34] Silber and Bhatt, 22-42.

[35] Sageman, 78-84.

[36] Borum, 78-96

[37] Gilles Kepel. *Jihad: The Trials of Political Islam.* (Translated by Al Roberts), (London, UK: Tauris & Co. Ltd., 2003), 26-41.

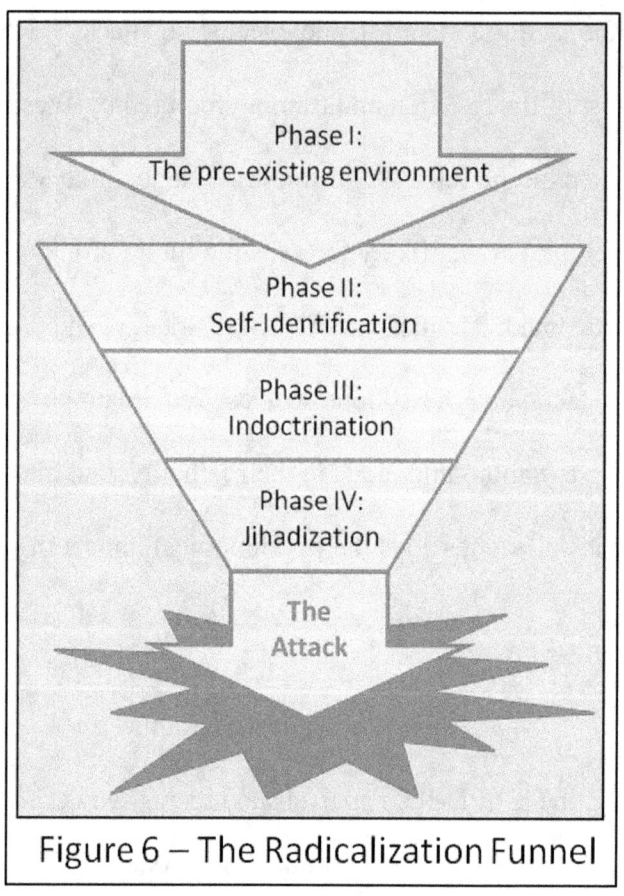

Figure 6 – The Radicalization Funnel [38]

As summarized previously, there are Quranic allowances (and requirements) for the support of Jihad: Jihad of the courts, Jihad of the Internet, and other forms of "struggle" which support the violent Jihadist directly or indirectly. Many would argue that a Jihad of the courts is being waged by the Muslim Brotherhood political refugee leadership[39] that populates the Council of American Islamic Relations (commonly known as CAIR). This organization continually conducts Islamist Jihad in the United States by producing misinformation and initiating legal attacks against individuals, schools, and government institutions who oppose their Islamist agenda under the banner of defending

---

[38] This graphic was created by the author in accord with the concepts provided by the referenced NYPD-IU report by Silber and Bhatt, 12-48.

[39] They are also unindicted co-conspirators of the first World Trade Center bombing. *Jihad Watch. Rep. King Demands Answers about non-Prosecution of Hamas-linked CAIR; CAIR's Hoomer Complains.* http://www.jihadwatch.org/cgi-sys/cgiwrap/br0nc0s/managed-mt/mt-search.cgi?search=unindicted+c oconspirators&IncludeBlogs=1&limit=20, (accessed February 15, 2013).

the faith.[40]  Often, because of limited resources, individuals and organization simply yield

to their demands instead of fighting CAIR in court.[41]  This alternative tactic is generically

referred to as "Jihad of the Pen[42] and appears difficult to oppose.

As for those who begin the radicalization process but never commit an attack,

studies show these individuals depart from the process for various reasons.[43]  Perhaps

they did not encounter the legitimizing personalities required, or they might have

personal relationships that normalized their worldview, thus preventing further

radicalization.  Psychological research confirms that an increased and positive interaction

with non-Muslims inhibits the radicalization process by intercepting the creation of the

dehumanized "other" within the mind of the would-be attacker.  It is not possible to know

how many begin the radicalization process and yet fall short of becoming operative

terrorists, but some percentage of a given population will constantly produce "seeking"

candidates who are subject to entering the process.[44]

Theory Proposal:  A Combined Radicalization Model

As documented above, the NYPD Phased Radicalization Model[45] provides

analysis with a framework for understanding the progressive nature of the psychological

advancement through the radicalization process.  It offers markers and a common lexicon

---

[40] Jihad Watch. *Muslim Brotherhood – ISNA Convention:  "Don't Talk to the FBI."*
http://www.jihadwatch.org/cgi-sys/cgiwrap/br0nc0s/managed-mt/mt-search.cgi?search=cair+islamis
t+objectives&IncludeBlogs=1&limit=20, (accessed February 15, 2013).

[41] Jihad Watch. *The Victimology Subterfuge.* http://www.jihadwatch.org/cgi-sys/cgiwrap/
br0nc0s/managed-mt/mt-search.cgi?search=Jihad+of+the+courts&IncludeBlogs=1&limit=20, (accessed
February 15, 2013).

[42] Heather Gregg.  "Fighting the Jihad of the Pen:  Countering Revolutionary Islam's Ideology."
*Terrorism and Political Violence* 22 (2010):  292-314.

[43] Silber and Bhatt, 12-48.

[44] Sageman, 58-78.

[45] Silber and Bhatt, 12-42.

for sharing data and understanding between security professionals. It introduces the concept of a Phase I: Pre-Existing Environment, but it neither explains nor explores in any detail what that population is. Aboul-Enein's discussion of Islamists[46] explains the source population, but does not proceed beyond the codification of Islamists into those who seek to obtain the Islamist end state through their personal conduct, political action, or violent militantism. Logic suggests the two models can be combined and ease the understanding of the overall Islamist radicalization process. (See Figure 7)

The combined model theory proposed[47] in Figure 7 depicts Sunni populations producing a yet undefined percentage of "seekers" on a reoccurring basis. The population source of these seekers establishes the unique Phase I Environment. As individual seekers begin their passage through the radicalization process, it is logical for each to modify their individual behavior in Phase II Self-Identification. Seekers might progress into political activism as the process takes them into Phase III Indoctrination. Some number of the seekers might then become militant as they move into the final Phase IV Jihadization. Within that Phase IV population, some number of those radicalized militants will execute attacks. Even the casual observer will note that the NYPD's phases and Aboul-Enein's population groups theory combine well, and the evolutionary nature of the process shown in the combined model is logical.

---

[46] Aboul-Enein, 24-42.

[47] Proposed and created by the author.

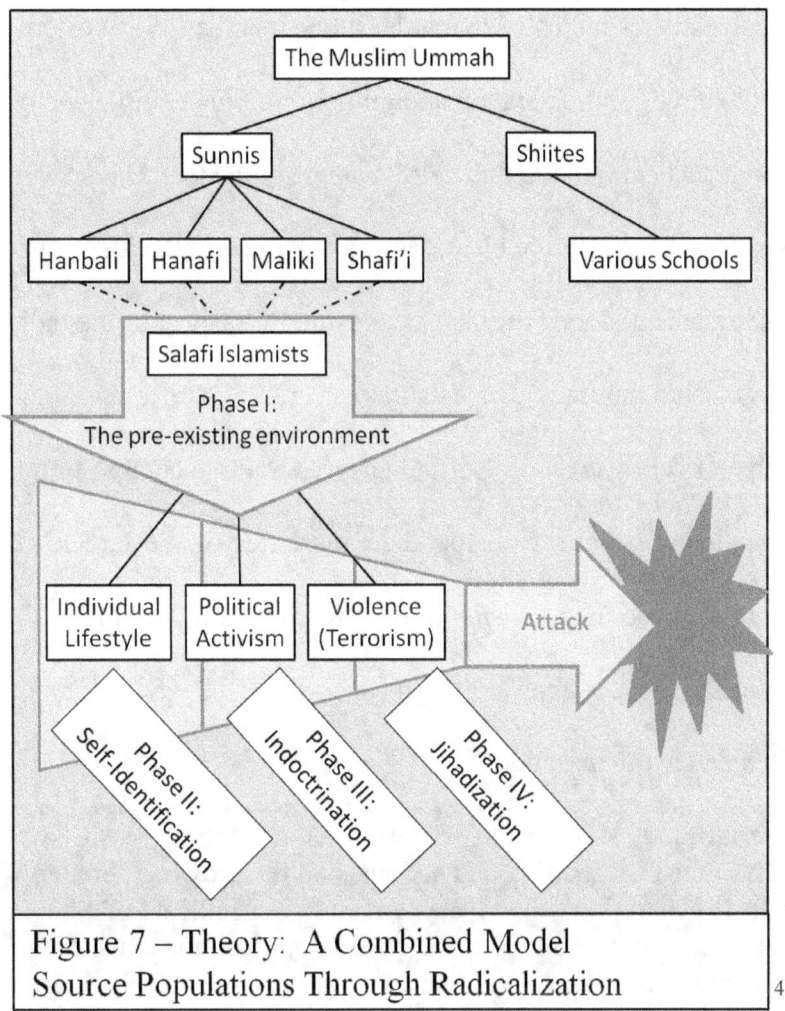

Figure 7 – Theory: A Combined Model
Source Populations Through Radicalization [48]

The Internet as a Virtual Terror Training Camp

This paper previously highlighted the evolving nature of terrorism and the types

of individuals who pose a threat to U.S. interests by categorizing the terrorists into three

groups: foreign with foreign support, domestic with foreign support, and domestic

without foreign support. The Jihadist war against the Soviet Union in Afghanistan played

a central role in the training of terrorists and taught an entire generation of Jihadi leaders

that Superpowers could be defeated by Jihadists, further encouraging their long-term

---

[48] The graphic was created by the author in order to propose a combined concept to visualize the
flow of terrorists from the source popultion through the radicalization process.

vision. Previously, studies indicated that at least one member of a Western terror cluster

needed to travel to a religious education and militant training camp, usually in Pakistan or

Yemen, to provide tactical training and gain strategic guidance. U.S. efforts to identify

the travel and intercept these future cluster leaders resulted in the identification and

disruption of many potential terror cells. As a result, this aspect of the radicalization

process was driven onto the Internet as Islamist terrorist organizations countered U.S.

efforts to seal the border by creating "virtual terrorist training camps" online.[49]

The transition of Islamist calls for Jihad, recruiting of Westerners already residing

within target countries and the provision of training resources is confirmed within many

U.S. Government reports. As an example and according to the Senate report, a July 2007

National Intelligence Estimate stated:

> The spread of radical–especially Salafi–Internet sites, increasingly
> aggressive anti-U.S. rhetoric and actions, and the growing number of
> radical, self-generating cells in Western countries indicate that the radical
> and violent segment of the West's Muslim population is expanding,
> including in the United States. The arrest and prosecution by U.S. law
> enforcement of a small number of violent Islamic extremists inside the
> United States–who are becoming more connected ideologically, virtually,
> and or in a physical sense to the global extremist movement–points to the
> possibility that others may become sufficiently radicalized that they will
> view the use of violence there as legitimate.[50]

In testimony before the Senate, then-Deputy Director of National Intelligence for

Analysis, Dr. Thomas Fingar, explained the linkage:

> The growing use of the Internet to identify and connect with networks
> throughout the world offers opportunities to build relationships and gain
> expertise that previously were available only in overseas training camps.
> It is likely that such independent groups will use information on

---

[49] U.S. Senate, 10-12.

[50] Ibid., 10.

destructive tactics available on the Internet to boost their own capabilities.[51]

As such, the Internet has become the most significant factor in the radicalization process.[52] In spite of this increasingly common conclusion, U.S. Senate and House Committee terror reports continue to show that current national security strategy is devoid of direction designed to counter the Islamists' strategy. The Bush-era National Implementation Plan recognized:

> Defeating terrorism, especially terrorism inspired by violent Islamist extremism, will require an array of government resources in addition to traditional classified counterterrorism tools and tactics by the intelligence and law enforcement communities.[53]

## Summary of Findings: Conclusions

The nation's security efforts must go beyond foreign intelligence and domestic law enforcement. The current U.S. strategy relies on uncoordinated community outreach activities and fragmented communications strategies. The results of the scientific studies summarized above show that the United States must isolate and discredit violent Islamist ideology by supporting non-Islamist Muslims while neutralizing Islamist recruiting mechanisms by aggressively countering their anti-U.S. propaganda as a source of grievance. Pro-U.S. information operations must improve perceptions of the U.S. "brand" by clarifying historic misinformation while advertising positive U.S. actions, particularly those actions within Muslim lands. The quiet diplomacy of the past where the United States felt no obligation to respond to negative propaganda is an outdated and obsolete form of thought. The silent moral high ground will not defuse the threat;

---

[51] U.S. Senate, 12.

[52] Sageman, 42-48.

[53] U.S. Senate, 10-15.

therefore, Islamist ideology on the Internet must be defeated by employing all of the instruments of national power as a priority objective within this Long War. Intelligence and law enforcement reports clearly indicate that the Internet continues to be used to spread the terrorists' message globally[54] in order to recruit and radicalize followers, and to provide training and targeting information for future attacks. Moreover, the U.S. Government cannot continue its strategy of hope for the interception of terrorist attacks just-in-time by intercepting radicals prior to the execution of their attacks while it rehearses for the mitigation of impending destruction. This "playing not to lose" strategy attempts to deal with the terrorist after his creation instead of preventing his development in the first place. If indeed the United States cannot kill and capture its way out of this war, then different strategies are required to reduce the output of the radicalization funnel as early in that process as possible.

---

[54] U.S. policy, strategy, and law should reflect the fact that the Internet resects no national border. As such, self-restraining U.S. counter-radicalization and counterterror actions through antiquated foreign and domestic definitions only exposes U.S. interests to greater risk.

# CHAPTER 5:  ISLAMIST GRAND STRATEGY

Know the enemy, know yourself; your victory will never be endangered.
Know the terrain, know the weather; your victory will then be total.[1]
                                                                    – Sun Tzu

United States (U.S.) national security officials entered the Bush-era's Global War on Terror (GWOT) with little understanding of Islam and virtually no understanding of Islamism.  Al-Qaeda might have played a leading role in the movement's global Jihad, but few officials knew what al-Qaeda was and even fewer still understood the Global Islamist Movement that had spent more than four decades refining its philosophy, training, and building an organization, and planning for the reestablishment of a true Islamic state.[2]  The attacks of 11 September 2001 were only one attack within a much larger war against the West and the United States, and were designed as part of a grand strategy to neutralize the world's sole remaining superpower, to cause the United States to withdraw its guardianship of world order, and to reclaim formerly Muslim lands from the ensuing chaos.[3]  Al-Qaeda might have conducted several attacks against the United States and Western interests, but al-Qaeda remains only one organization within the greater Global Islamist Movement.[4]  Although not readily apparent to the common American, the movement has global leaders, strategists, and a grand strategic thought, all of which are designed to further Islamist objectives.

---

[1] Sun Tzu, 129.

[2] Mehar Omar Khan, "Is There an Islamic Way of War?" *The Small Wars Journal.* (2010) http://small warsjournal.com/blog/2010/03/is-there-an-islamic-way-of-war/, (accessed February 15, 2013).

[3] Khalil, 1-7.

[4] Since 11 September, the apparent and exponential spread of al-Qaeda is largely an illusion and a result of disparate Islamist movements capitalizing on al-Qaeda's perceived fame to improve their own stature, recruiting, and fund raising.

Islamism is the ultra-fundamentalist movement that seeks to create and enforce a more strict observance of Islam in all aspects of life including political, social, and economic based on Sharia law. As discussed in Chapter 2, legal meaning (or Sharia) is derived from the Quran, the Hadith, scholarly writings, and legal precedence. Islamists seek to remove "modern innovations" which they view as corrupting influences upon Muslims. Islamists reject modern forms of government (including democracies and republics) and reject peaceful methods as too slow; only armed action through Jihad is an acceptable way to achieve political power.[5]

## Leaders of the Global Islamist Resurgence

The current Islamist resurgence is not a new phenomenon: it has been building for decades. As introduced above, Islamist doctrines have been developing for centuries, and their refinement and manipulation continues today. The Egyptian Hassan al-Banna (1906-1949), the founder of the Muslim Brotherhood in 1928, was a social activist writing about colonialism, socialism, and Islamic society.[6] Al-Banna's legacy includes his impact on modern Islamist though his protégé, Sayeed Qutb.[7] Qutb (1906-1966) was an Egyptian author, Islamist theorist, and leading member of the Muslim Brotherhood following al-Banna's assassination. Qutb was an educator and traveled to the West and United States where he experienced and condemned Western culture, secular society, and

---

[5] Khalil, 1-7.

[6] Bernard Lewis, *The Crisis of Islam: Holy War and Unholy Terror.* (New York, NY: The Modern Library, 2003), 20-122..

[7] Qutb is a significant figure in the evolution of thought within the modern Global Islamist Movement and modern terrorism designed to weaken local regimes by targeting their Western supporters for asymmetric attacks. Some (Sageman, Berringer, and others) recommend separating Bin Laden and his ilk from the Muslim masses by branding them "Qutb'ists." The intent of such an act would be to remove religious legitimacy and imply cult-of-personality status on the followers of Qutb. Such nuance has value.

democracy for their corrupt and Godless natures. He is best known for his writing on political Islam, social justice and, most relevant to this work, the book entitled *Milestones*. *Milestones* remains an influential Islamist political, religious and social manifesto, and includes a key chapter which advocates for a couple of enduring revolutionary concepts including: (1) revolutionary change should be led by a Jihadi vanguard representing the greater Muslim community; and (2) the eventual destruction of corrupt Arab puppet regimes by first separating them from their colonial puppet masters. Qutb recognized that Islamists could never defeat local secular rulers as long as they enjoyed Western support; therefore, their Jihadi blows needed to target the colonialists first. Further, Qutb recognized that modern transportation made the colonial powers vulnerable to asymmetric attacks globally. Sayeed Qutb spent the latter years of his life writing from an Egyptian prison before he was executed in 1966 for treason. His Quranic commentary, *In the Shade of the Quran*, is also widely translated, available on the Internet, and commonly informs Islamist thought. Sayeed Qutb's brother Mohammad fled to Saudi Arabia where he became a professor of Islamic Studies in Saudi Arabia's influential (and Islamist) King Abdul-Aziz University, where he trained future Jihadi leaders including Ayman al-Zawahiri, Mafouz Azzam, and Osama bin Laden.[8]

The Palestinian Mafouz Azzam (born 1941) was a close friend of Mohammad Qutb. He was an early member of the Muslim Brotherhood and founder of Hamas. He viewed the 1967 Arab-Israeli War as an Arab disgrace, which discredited the secular Pan-Arab movement as impotent and as the final proof of secular failure. In 1974, Azzam graduated from Cairo's famed Islamic university, al-Azhar, with a PhD in Islamic

---

[8] Lewis, 34-88.

Jurisprudence, providing him with academic Islamic legitimacy. Azzam's writings clearly stated his Quranic interpretation that the Jihad is defined as holy war only and not as "struggle." He wrote that Jihad is a collective obligation on all and is not "optional."[9] He is known as the spiritual father of al-Qaeda and is credited with discovering Osama bin Laden and bringing him to Afghanistan during the Soviet-Afghan War. Azzam was one of the first to realize that radicalized Arab fighters traveling unaided to Pakistan for Jihad were being "dumped" in Pakistan where they attempted, without coordination, to make their way into Afghanistan for anti-Soviet Jihad.[10] Azzam returned to Pakistan and, as the Muslim Brotherhood's representative there, addressed the need to support the flow of Jihadist Arab fighters into Afghanistan. Al-Qaeda was founded by him as al-Qaeda al-Sulba,[11] or "a firm foundation"–that is, a foundation (or institute) for proper and pious Islam. Azzam's nephew was Ayman al-Zawahiri (born 1951) whose Jihadist career includes the 1981 assassination of Egyptian President Anwar Sadat, the bombings of U.S. embassies, and fighting the U.S.-led coalition in Afghanistan. Al-Zawahiri coauthored bin Laden's Fatwa[12] declaring war against the United States[13] and, in 2011, he assumed command of al-Qaeda following the death of Osama bin Laden.

---

[9] Within accepted Quranic writings Jihad is discussed as warfare with two forms: optional and mandatory. Optional is described as mandatory, but only until there are "enough" Jihadists. Mandatory is described as required upon everyone. The clear definitional problem is discerning what are the differences in circumstances which separate optional and mandatory, and the defining of how much Jihad is enough Jihad?

[10] Jim Lacey, *A Terrorist's Call to Global Jihad: Deciphering Abu Musab Al-Suri's Islamic Jihad Manifesto.* (Annapolis, MD: Naval Institute Press, 2008): 8-32.

[11] Al-Qaeda is commonly mistranslated as "the base" or "the headquarters" in error. The evolution of the name is correctly noted herein. If al-Qaeda were intended as a stand-alone term, these mistranslations would be accurate, but the entire original term is al-Qaeda al-Sulba which is clearly "a firm foundation" as in a charitable foundation.

[12] Fatwa is defined as a religiously supported decree, an informed decision following a line of Quranic jurisprudence thought which supports the argument with the holy texts, precedence and logic. Traditionally, only a person having the education and certification of a Mufti can issue a Fatwa, which

## Abu Musab al-Suri:[14]  The Clausewitz of Islam

A twenty-first century Salafist named Abu Musab al-Suri wrote several books that are central to current Jihadist thought and is considered by Islamists as "the Clausewitz for the modern Jihadi movement." His writings represent grand strategy for the Global Jihadist Movement and are readily available on the Internet for global consumption. Just like the writings of bin Laden, Qutb, and others, al-Suri's writings perpetually influence new generations of potential Islamist terrorists through the radicalization process.[15] Al-Suri studied in detail the writings of various Western classical strategists including Carl von Clausewitz, Samuel Huntington, and even President Richard Nixon. He repeatedly notes that Huntington's *Clash of Civilizations* had a significant impact on his thinking, particularly as it relates to building an "us-versus-them" perception to divide the Muslim population away from Western influences. He stressed the need to bring Huntington's epic clash of civilizations into effect so that the two worlds will be divided, not united. Throughout his writings, he uses *Clash of Civilizations* and other similar books to prove to his readership that the West remains an enduring threat to Muslims. Al-Suri assessed U.S. regional policy as "an American led campaign against the Arab and Islamic world" with clear objectives for the "elimination of the civilizational, religious, political, economic, social, and cultural existence of Muslims."[16] As a result, all Western actions

---

neither al-Zawahri or Bin-Laden possessed. Theoretically, they exceeded their Islamic authority and should have been branded as heretics for their "innovation," but were not.

[13] Khalil, 22-32.

[14] Al-Suri is the nom de guerre for the Syrian born terror theorist Mustafa Setmariam Nasar. Litterally, al-Suri means "The Syrian."

[15] Lacey, 112-132.

[16] Ibid., 164.

are viewed in light of that suspicion which feeds directly into the struggle for perceived legitimacy.[17]

Al-Suri builds upon the writings of other Islamists from the fourteenth-century scholars who called for and Quranically-justified defensive Jihad against Mongol and Tartar invaders. Because of that work, and its inculcation into following writings like those of al-Suri, those interpretations of Jihad remain today. Al-Suri also built on Sayeed Qutb's idea, who called for Jihad in defense of the Ummah. Qutb viewed not only the presence of Westerners, but also Western influence, Western products, Western businesses and such as contaminating to Muslim culture. Qutb concluded that all Western influence was corrupt, that it represented an attack of Western culture upon Muslim culture, and that these aggressions required an armed response in defense of Muslims. Al-Suri built upon that foundation.

In his books, al-Suri conducts a historic review of the current global Islamic resurgence and identifies three waves of Jihadi fervor that started in the 1960s and continues to build today. Understanding these three waves is informative in understanding the current Global Jihadist Movement. They are defined as being members of time-phased populations of participants in the Modern Islamist [Jihadi] Movement, as follows:

- The first population includes those "founders" in the 1960s, such as Sayeed Qutb and Anwar al-Awlaki, who were instrumental in starting the current movement.

- The second population fought, gained experience, and solidified the movement during the Soviet-Afghan War years, continued through wars in Bosnia, Chechnya, Kashmir, and the like, and ended with the 11 September 2001 World

[17] Nacos, 78-142.

Trade Center attack. This period gave rise to new household names including Osama bin Laden.

- The final period begins with the 9/11 attacks but is significantly shaped by the U.S.-led Global War on Terror (GWOT). The individuals defined in this period include, primarily, Jihadi veterans of Iraq, Afghanistan, Yemen, and Somalia.

During the first wave, Qutb built on the philosophical works of others, but his book *Milestones* changed the strategy for the struggle for Arab/Muslim independence from the Western imperial powers and their puppet governments. Qutb called for Jihadists not to fight the corrupt local governments, but instead to separate the puppet from its puppet master by attacking the puppet master directly. Using airplanes and international travel, Qutb realized that a select few fighters could take the fight to the puppet master. He calculated that the imperial powers were pain-averse and would quickly retreat from the region when bloodied.[18] Al-Suri noted that Qutb's wave established the strategic framework for the Global Jihadist Movement.

During the second wave, Saudi oil money combined with under-employed but growing populations and an unexpected opportunity to fight a proxy Cold War in Afghanistan to create a global cadre of experienced, trained, and radicalized fighters who were prepared to continue the Jihad in their home countries. When the Soviets retreated from Afghanistan, Arab Jihadists had three options: some simply returned home; however, many were wanted as criminals in their home countries and could not return home. Those fighters either married local females to start families in Pakistan or

---

[18] This paradigm also matches U.S. reactions to terror attacks in the Middle East and Africa over recent decades. U.S. actions reinforced Qutb's paradigm which, it can be argued, encourages future additional attacks.

Afghanistan or they became wanted criminals hiding within the dark underbelly of the Global Islamist Movement's network of experienced Jihadists. This proliferation of militant radicals immediately destabilized their home countries, which were ill-prepared to receive and reintegrate the radicals into their home societies.[19]

## Combatants vs. Non-Combatants

In al-Suri's writings, he notes a key nuance within Islamic law that does not denote a difference between members of the military and civilians; rather, it distinguishes combatants from non-combatants. Westerners commonly define a combatant as someone who is actively fighting while, in Islam, a combatant is also a person who fights or assists in the fight with their wealth or moral support. Islam provides for other forms of Holy War including the use of courts, propaganda, and even the U.S. Government's own complaint system.[20] This is a crucial finding which al-Suri uses to judge the West, and Americans in particular, are all guilty of aggression against Muslims; therefore, they are all combatants. This is because the American people:

- elect rulers who decide policies which are against Muslims;

- pay taxes which fund "campaigns of aggression" against Muslims;

- supply resources for aggression against Muslims;

- supply the security agencies that seek to harm Muslims.

---

[19] Lacey, 155.

[20] The U.S.-based Islamist organization CAIR continues to target anti-Islamist efforts as racist bigots in the courts, in the media and within the Department of Defense's (DoD's) own Inspector General investigative organizations. This form of pressure to further the Islamist cause is known as Jihad of the courts and continues to have a significant impact upon open and completely honest discourse on these sensitive national security issues. CAIR leadership is populated with Muslim Brotherhood political refugees and includes unindicted co-conspirators in the 1995 bombing of the World Trade Center.

Even opponents of U.S. policies are deemed "combatants against Islam" and are equally

guilty because they passively support the U.S. Government by paying their taxes,

providing information, and so forth. Because these acts constitute attacks and/or

aggression against the Ummah, a defensive Jihad is required and all American property,

all American institutions, and all American individuals are judged as targets because they

each, collectively and individually, are guilty of aggression against the global Muslim

community.[21]

## Unifying Effort

The long-game goal of the Global Jihadist Movement, after ejecting the Western

"occupiers" from the Middle East, is the establishment of an Islamic Emirate as a starting

point to defend Islam, to defend Muslims, and as an initial step toward the reviving the

Caliphate. Al-Suri reminds "field leaders" that they must not lose sight of their strategic

goals by overreacting to localized events and warns them not to become involved in "side

battles" which divert from this strategic goal. He calls for Jihadists to have patience, and

warns Jihadi leaders that their younger supporters might display a zeal for combat that is

counterproductive to their strategic ends and must be moderated by the wisdom and

experience of the elders. He defines the need for enduring unity of effort through

commitment and patience as their core strategy.[22]

## Popular Support: Hearts and Minds of the Population

Al-Suri assessed the condition of the Muslim population (Ummah) as being in a

state of foment caused by external (Western) attack and internal (illegitimate local

---

[21] Lacey, 160-172.

[22] Ibid., 169-170.

government) misery. He cites these pressures and suffering as proof that the modern

alternative to the Islamic Caliphate has failed; therefore, the Caliphate must be restored.

He states the belief that a militant vanguard of the Ummah must take advantage of these

conditions and turn the power of the people into an active and effective vehicle for

change. Al-Suri acknowledged that the Global Jihadi Movement could not overturn local

governments or replace them with Islamic emirates without the support of the local

populations. Al-Suri stressed that this is a long-term struggle and could require

generations to complete. He continued, "Therefore this Jihad cannot be engaged in

isolation from the Ummah, or as its proxy. Rather, the current Jihad represents the

vanguard of this blessed Ummah."[23]

Al-Suri's strategic guidance appears in sync with U.S. counterinsurgency doctrine

where the struggle for legitimacy within the eyes of the population remains the center of

gravity.[24] The real struggle is for the support of the population. The problem as seen by

Jihadist strategists is that only a small percentage of the population is mobilized for Jihad.

So, they wonder, how do we mobilize the greater population? Al-Suri answers by stating

that a fighting creed must be firmly established and clarified in order to attain a

"Revolutionary Jihadist Climate" which gives spontaneous rise to the means for Jihad

within that individual. He stated, "Violent Jihad is an individual duty obligatory upon

every Muslim."

---

[23] Lacey, 161.

[24] U.S. Marine Corps, *Small Wars Manual.* (1940), http://www.au.af.mil/au/awc/awcgate/swm/index.htm, (accessed October 4, 2012).

Al-Suri describes his vision of the individual radicalization process as including three well-defined stages. Those stages are[25]

- discovering an Islamist Sentiment: what does it meant to be a "good Muslim;"

- building a will to fight: the maturation of the Islamist sentiment; and

- instilling the Jihadist Creed: nurtured through education and instruction.[26]

Al-Suri's stages of Jihadist development would logically exist in potential recruits globally, including those within the West. The identifiable manifestations of these three steps might be enlightening for U.S. security personnel who seek to identify and interdict the process, thereby preventing a terror event.

## Islamist View of Western Democracy

Fundamentalists around the globe reject democracy as a Western innovation and alien to Islam. Democracy is a creation of the infidel Western political system and places the judgments of men above God's dictates.[27] Democratic traditions exclude Allah, Muhammad, or the Quran. This attitude was cemented into Salafist beliefs by the founders of modern Islamic radicalism Hassan al-Banna, Abu al-Mououdi, and Sayeed Qutb. Islamist scholars and bloggers continue to build on the writings of these men and continue their themes uninterrupted. Highlights of their writings (backed by Quranic quotations) include:

- "Allah is the creator, and the right to rule belongs to him."

---

[25] U.S. Defense Intelligence Agency, *Abu Musab Al-Suri. The Clausewitz of Al-Qaida Ideology. Twenty-First Century Al-Qaida Strategist.* (Norfolk, VA: US Navy, Visual Information Directorate, 2009).

[26] Lacey, 168.

[27] Mark Gabriel, *Culture Clash: Islam's War on the West.* (Lake Mary, FL: Front Line Publishing, A Strang Company, 2007): 12-44.

- "Democracy violates Islamic law because it steals the right to rule away from Allah and gives it to people."
- "Those who accept any political system that does not come from Islam have left the faith and will be rejected by Allah."[28]

In stark contrast and as an example of the cross-cultural miscommunication which needlessly enflames Islamists, in 2005 the U.S. Secretary of State, Condoleezza Rice, gave a speech at Cairo's American University in which she stated a new U.S. policy:[29]

> We should all look to a future when every government respects the will of its citizens–because the ideal of democracy is universal. For 60 years, my country, the United States, pursued stability at the expense of democracy in this region here in the Middle East–and we achieved neither. Now, we are taking a different course. We are supporting the democratic aspirations of all people . . .
>
> We know these advances will not come easily, or all at once. We know that different societies will find forms of democracy that work for them. When we talk about democracy, though, we are referring to governments that protect certain basic rights for all their citizens–among these, the right to speak freely; the right to associate; the right to worship as you wish; the right to educate your children–boys and girls; and freedom from the midnight knock of the secret police.
>
> Securing these rights is the hope of every citizen, and the duty of every government.[30]
>
> – Condoleezza Rice

Us-versus-Them: The Dehumanization of "the Other"

All unbelieving non-Muslims are characterized as impure, inferior, untrustworthy, trying to destroy Islam itself, and as the enemy of all Muslims. Because non-Muslims are judged as impure, they are not allowed by the Quran (Surah 9:28) to be near the sacred

---

[28] Gabriel, 32-36.

[29] Although the intent of the administration's position is understandable, careful rewording could have produced the same meaning with less inflammatory wording. As an example, "representative government" or "a government representing the will of the people" might have replaced the often inflammatory word "democracy."

[30] Gabriel, 32-44.

cities of Mecca and Medina in Saudi Arabia's Hejaz region. Because non-Muslims are impure, the Quran tells Muslims to view themselves as superior to all other peoples of the world.[31] According to the Quran:

> You are the best of the nations raised up for the benefit of men; you enjoy what is right and forbid the wrong and believe in Allah; and if the followers of the Book [Christians and Jews] had believed, it would have been better for them; of them, some are believers and most of them are transgressors. (Surah 3:110)[32]

> Believe no one unless he follows your religion. True Guidance is the guidance of Allah. (Surah 3.73)[33]

> O ye who believe! Take not unto your intimacy those outside your ranks: they will not fail to corrupt you. They only desire your ruin; rank hatred has already appeared from their mouths: what their hearts conceal is far worse. We made plain to you the signs, if you have wisdom. (Surah 3:118)[34]

> O ye who believe! Take not the Jew and the Christians for your friends and protectors: they are but friends and protectors of each other. And he amongst you that turns to them is of them. Verily Allah guideth not a people unjust. (Surah 5:51)[35]

In light of these scriptures, it is not surprising that Islamists, with their literalist interpretation of the Quran, seek to segregate themselves from non-Muslims. Further, these scriptures advance the psychological separation required in the dehumanizing "us-vs.-them" phase of the radicalization process that leads to a terroristic attack.

> You shall not find a people who believe in Allah and the latter day befriending those who act in opposition to Allah and His Messenger, even

---

[31]Gabriel, 28-32.

[32] Ali, *The Quran,* 155.

[33] Ibid., 146.

[34] Ibid., 157.

[35] Ibid., 264-265.

though they were their own fathers, or their sons, or their brothers, or their
kinsfolk . . .                                                        (Surah 58:22)[36]


O ye who believe!  Take not for protectors your fathers and your brothers
if they love infidelity above faith; if any of you do so, they are wrong.
                                                                     (Surah 9:23)[37]


Verses like these encourage separation between Muslims and non-Muslims, and

simplify the psychological creation of "the other" within that isolated community.  For

the radicalizing Islamist, this includes isolation likely includes family members and

mosques because they are judged as "not Muslim enough."[38]

---

[36] Ali, *The Quran,* 1439.

[37] Ibid., 443.

[38] Gabriel, 32-44.

## CHAPTER 6:  UNITED STATES (U.S.) COUNTERTERROR STRATEGY

> The Islamic Movement openly broadcasts its intent.  There is no "conspiracy."  However, because the U.S. security strategy apparatus is operating on the basis of a strategic pseudo-reality, they are unable to connect the dots and correlate the fact.  Strategic analysts are unable to identify the threat or deduce the Islamic Movement's collective doctrine and strategy.
>
> – Colonel Richard Higgins

The December 2011 U.S. Senate's Homeland Security Committee hearing report on Islamist Radicalization concluded that there is a "dominant threat" to the military which is both "persistent and enduring," and that the threat of home-grown terror continues to increase.[1]  In August 2011, the White House released a report about its efforts to counter homegrown terrorist acts inside the United States.  The eight-page document highlighted community engagement as the key component of the administration's counter-radicalization and counterterrorism efforts.  Following the President's report, members of the House Homeland Security Committee issued a joint statement expressing disapproval of the Administration's strategy, citing three major flaws:  (1) a failure to identify violent Islamist ideology as the root cause of homegrown terrorism; (2) a failure to address the Internet's role in radicalization; and (3) a failure to advance more robust strategy to counter the threat.[2]  Only an investigation of the family of policy documents can determine if the charges are founded or not.

### Literature Review:  U.S. National Security Policies

Thus far, this work has focused on interpreting, explaining, and assessing the Islamist threat.  That threat could be defined as establishing the requirement against

---

[1] U.S. Senate, 3-8.

[2] U.S. House, 1-2.

which U.S. strategists should be planning; however, planners only plan against established political requirements or statements of policy. It is, therefore, appropriate that this body of work must include a literature review of U.S. national policy and the supporting guidance and documents. As noted throughout this work, the battle for the hearts and minds of would-be terrorists is being fought (or should be fought) in large part on the Internet; therefore, only unclassified, publically available U.S. policy and guidance documents will be assessed. Although analysis of classified policy/strategy documents would undoubtedly be enlightening, such is beyond the scope of this work. Thus, this effort constrains itself to unclassified Obama-era policy and strategy documents, and focuses on the guidance directing current planning efforts. Selected Bush-era documents have been reviewed for comparison and contrast, and as a means to demonstrate the current administration's shift in national focus in order to underscore this author's observation that national leadership has shifted away from counterterrorism as a policy.

The literature review that follows starts at the top with the U.S. National Security Strategy (NSS) and cascades down the hierarchy of guidance documents to lower level products. Although most subdivisions within the U.S. Government (USG) publish similar subordinate strategies, this review is restricted to the USG departments primarily charged with matters of national security; therefore, only Presidential, Department of State (DoS), Department of Defense (DoD) and Department of Homeland Security (DHS) documents are assessed. The policy reviews which follow are restrained to seek specific wording applicable to terrorism, an understanding of Islamist ideology, and the Global Islamist Movement. This limitation is emplaced because of the understanding that senior-level policy statements drive subordinate planners and resources; without guidance, the attention and resources of subordinate organizations will drift away from this problem.

### U.S. National Security Strategy: The Obama Administration

The Presidential NSS is the basic national document that drives all subordinate policy and/or strategy documents. The most recent NSS was published in May of 2010; it will continue to form U.S. policy until abrogated by other statements of policy or replaced by a future NSS. Because an NSS is the formative document of USG policy, assessing it with regard to the threat of Islamist terrorism is an important component of this thesis. Within the body of the current document, the NSS discusses terrorism and terrorist threats in two environments–domestic and international. It does so logically and adheres to the legal division of responsibilities and authorities within U.S. Code. Restrictions, if any exist in this formulation, are beyond the scope of this thesis, which is to investigate the threat of the Global Islamist Movement and actions taken to counter it. Thus, the entire body of the current NSS is measured against the global terrorism threat.

### *Strengthening Security and Resilience at Home*

In the sub-chapter discussion of homeland defense, the NSS expresses the President's domestic counterterror strategy as designed to "empower communities" to counter radicalization at home. The NSS specifies that that the best defense strategy against the threat of domestically radicalized attackers is "well informed and equipped families, local communities, and institutions."[3] It directs the USG to invest in intelligence and "empower local communities" through cooperation. In terminology, it

---

[3] U.S. President. *National Security Strategy.* (Washington, DC: Government Printing Office, May 2010.): 19-20.

focuses its wording on reaction to terror events, building community (victim) resiliency and governmental response after the attacks. It fails to address interruption of the radicalization process or prevention of domestic terror attacks by Islamists.

*Disrupt, Dismantle, and Defeat al-Qa'ida[4] and Violent Extremist Affiliates in Afghanistan, Pakistan and Around the World*

> Success requires a broad, sustained, and integrated campaign that judiciously applies every tool of American power–both military and civilian–as well as the concerted effort of like-minded states and multilateral institutions.
>
> We will always seek to delegitimize the use of terrorism and to isolate those who carry it out. Yet this is not global war against a tactic–terrorism or a religion–Islam. We are at war with a specific network, al-Qa'ida, and its terrorist affiliates who support efforts to attack the United States, our allies, and partners.[5]

This sub-chapter of the NSS specifies that the USG is waging a global campaign against al-Qaeda and its affiliates by denying them refuge and protecting the homeland. However, a global campaign against al-Qaeda falls well short of being a global war against the Global Islamist Movement that seeks the destruction of the United States.

The NSS concludes with summary statements of USG strategic objectives to deny al-Qaeda the ability to threaten Americans or our global interests by (1) denying them the use of safe havens, (2) denying them access to weapons of mass destruction, and (3) delivering "swift and sure" justice (through U.S. courts) where appropriate, and concludes with the policy statement that:

---

[4] USG policy/strategy documents rarely mention Islam or the Islamists by name, usually referring to the concepts though one organizational title "al-Qa'ida." Often, in transliteration, the term becomes one of the many variants existent throughout USG documents. This author prefers the most common form - "al-Qaeda". However, because the spelling used and context of any quote are precisely copied, some variants of al-Qa'ida, and other names, appear herein.

[5] U.S. President, *NSS,* 19.

Finally, we reject the notion that al-Qa'ida represents any religious authority. They are not religious leaders, they are killers: and neither Islam nor any other religion condones the slaughter of innocents.[6]

Critique: The very title subliminally suggests that the sub-chapter is only applicable to al-Qaeda in Afghanistan and Pakistan. It seems to downplay non-al-Qaeda organizations (like the Taliban) in Afghanistan and Pakistan and down plays al-Qaeda outside of Afghanistan and Pakistan. In view of (1) public presidential statements constantly claiming that al-Qaeda is all but destroyed, and (2) that the United States has been directed to extract itself from Afghanistan by 2014, this section of NSS "guidance" appears overcome by events and of little value to national security strategists. The section fails to mention Islamists and/or their radical ideology; while it does mention "Islam," it is done only in an apologetic manner.

### Strategic Communications

Within a discussion of whole government approaches, the NSS includes a short discussion on strategic communications wherein it specifies the necessity for unified strategic communications as essential for sustained global legitimacy. It highlights the imperative to "understanding the attitudes, opinions, grievances, and concerns of the people–not just the elites–around the world" as an enabler for representing the U.S. message with clearly and consistency.[7] The NSS does include a statement of values that support a strategic communications campaign targeting perceived foreign grievances:

> The United States believes certain values are universal and will work to promote them worldwide. These include an individual's freedom to speak

---

[6] Although this is a quote from the NSS, Islamist scholars (and the Islamists themselves) would argue with the assessment. The effort to separate the Islamists from the greater Muslim population supports psychological findings discussed in earlier chapters. U.S. President, *NSS,* 22.

[7] U.S. President, *NSS,* 16.

their mind, assemble without fear, worship as they please and choose their own leaders; they also include dignity, tolerance, and equality among all people, and the fair and equitable administration of justice.[8]

Critique: The NSS sections that reference domestic and international terrorism are but a very limited portion of the 52-page document's overall content. The NSS does recognize violent extremism as a continuing threat to the U.S. homeland and to its interests globally; further, it identifies the operational environment as "increasingly lethal" and "irregular." Presidential strategy correctly claims that al-Qaeda is "weakened," but fails to acknowledge other operational elements within the greater Global Islamist Movement. It mentions the "Arab awakening" (more commonly known as the Arab Spring) as a "change," but fails to codify the exact nature of the change.[9] In summary, the existing NSS fails to identify the threat with adequate specificity to drive subordinate USG policies and/or strategies.

U.S. National Strategy for Counterterrorism: The Obama Administration

On 28 June 2011 President Obama signed the National Strategy for Counterterrorism (NSCT) into effect with an opening reference to the "war against al-Qa'ida" and a call for "rededication" toward "meeting the challenges that remain." Of counterterror documents the targeted by this analysis for study, this NSCT is potentially the most useful of the U.S. strategy/policy documents remaining in effect. It is organized with an overview of U.S. counterterrorism strategy, the threat, U.S. guiding principles,

---

[8] Ibid., 35.

[9] Although too early to judge, it is easy to conceive that the Islamist Muslim Brotherhood or other anti-U.S. groups could seize power in Egypt or other Muslim majority nations. In such case U.S. influence would be weakened and threats to our national security and that of our allies would likely increase in number and severity. Early indications of a Western liberal democracy being successfully transplanted into the Middle East through these popular uprisings simply do not exist. Instead, the Islamists appear to be ascending to the fore.

goals, areas of focus, and concerns. The short 19-page document concludes that "AQ is on the path to defeat" and touts the death of Osama bin Laden in multiple places, but continues to discuss counterterrorism in far detail than does the President's NSS.

The President's NSCT strategy calls for maintaining pressure on al-Qaeda's "core" while emphasizing the "need for building partnerships and capacity, and our resilience." It also specifies, "Our strategy augments our focus on confronting the al-Qai'da-linked threats that continue to energy beyond its core safe haven in South Asia." This statement pays vague homage to the fact that the Islamist "starfish" known as al-Qa'ida is now scattered throughout the northern African, Asia, and beyond, and is no longer consolidated in Afghanistan-Pakistan, but without overtly stating so. It references the USG's "enduring approach to counterterrorism," but fails to specify what is (or has been) enduring about the U.S. approach. Instead, it repeats phases calling for the United States to "disrupt, dismantle, defeat al-Qa'ida" by using "every element of national power" in vague terms.[10]

The overarching goals within the NSCT articulate national desired CT end states; to protect the American people, the homeland, and American interests:

- disrupt, degrade, dismantle and defeat al-Qaeda and its affiliates and adherents;

- prevent terrorist development, acquisition and use of weapons of mass destruction;

- eliminate safe havens;

- build enduring counterterrorism partnerships and capabilities;

- degrade the linkage between al-Qaeda and its affiliates and adherents;

---

[10] U.S. President. *National Strategy for Counterterrorism.* (Washington, DC: Government Printing Office, 2011): 1.

- counter al-Qaeda ideology and its resonance, and diminish the specific drivers of violence that al-Qaeda exploits; and,

- deprive terrorists of their enabling means.[11]

Clearly, the final two are most impactful from the perspective of this thesis because they seek to counter al-Qaeda's ideology and de-link the organization from popular support: legal and illegal. The Areas of Focus listed within the strategy are a logical[12] discussion of specific regions and al-Qaeda affiliate groups which the strategy prioritizes for effort. The established Core Principles within the strategy are:

- adhering to U.S. core values;

- building security partnerships, applying CT tools and capabilities appropriately;

- building a culture of resilience.[13]

The NSCT acknowledges the connection between localized perceptions, grievances, and the individual's historic and political worldview; it specifies the countering of this "ideology" as the essential element of the strategy. It clarifies the U.S. position that "The U.S. deliberately uses the word 'war' to describe our relentless campaign against al-Qa'ida: however, this Administration has made it clear that we are not at war with the tactic of terrorism or the religion of Islam. We are at war with a specific organization."[14] The statement that "Our support for the aspirations of people throughout the Middle East, North Africa, and around the world to live in peace and

---

[11] U.S. President, *NSCT,* 8-11.

[12] Ibid., 13-14.

[13] The NSCT uses various forms of the word resilience which resilience is generally used to define an individual or group's ability and/or preparation to absorb or cope with the injury of an attack; therefore, resiliency is always reactive. This author work calls for proactive measures to prevent attacks by preventing the creation of the terrorist and not simply getting better at reaction the damage they cause.

[14] U.S. President, *NSCT,* 2.

prosperity under representative governments stands in marked contrast to al-Qa'ida's

dark and bankrupt worldview,"[15] and many others like it, are of great potential value in

the U.S. strategic communications effort.

> In this strategy, we have redoubled our efforts to undercut the resonance
> of the al-Qa'ida message while addressing those specific drivers of
> violence that al-Qa'ida exploits to recruit and motivate new generations of
> terrorists.[16]

Within the section titled *Information and Ideas: Al-Qa'ida Ideology, Messaging*

*and Resonance,* the NSCT clarifies that "this area underscores the importance of the

global information and ideas environment, which often involves unique challenges

requiring specialized CT approaches."[17]  This section of the document correctly identifies

the use of traditional media and cyberspace to undermine and inhibit their ideology while

diminishing their recruiting mechanisms.  It adds that "We must also put forward a

positive version of engagement with Muslim communities around the world so that we

are contrasting our vision of the future we are trying to build with al-Qa'ida's focus on

what it aims to destroy."  The document avoids the use of the term Islam other than to

state carefully that the U.S. is not at war with Islam.  It continues to use "al-Qa'ida's

ideology" as a euphemism for Islamist ideology and adds to the CT lexicon by codifying

the term "al-Qa'ida, its affiliates and adherents" (or AQAA)[18] as a new term of art.[19]

---

[15] Ibid., 1.

[16] Ibid., 19.

[17] Ibid., 17.

[18] According to the NSCT:  *Affiliates* is not a legal term of art; although it includes *Associated Forces*, it additionally includes groups and individuals against whom the United States is not authorized to use force based on the authorities granted by the Authorization for the Use of Military Force, Pub.L.107-40, 115 Stat.224 (2001).  The use of *Affiliates* in the strategy is intended to reflect a broader category of entities against whom the U.S. must bring various elements of national power, as appropriate and consistent with the law, to counter the threat they pose.  *Associated Forces* is a legal term of art that refers to cobelligerents of al-Qaeda or the Taliban against whom the President is authorized to use force (including

Within the strategy, the President acknowledges that "We continue to face a significant terrorist threat from al-Qa'ida, its affiliates, and its adherents," and that these organizations continue to make deliberate efforts to inspire individuals inside the U.S. to conduct "attacks on their own."[20] The only reference to "Muslim" is within the context of al-Qaeda's victims and avoids the fact that al-Qaeda is an Islamist terrorist organization populated by Muslims.

Critique: The NSCT is short and adds supportive words. Like all other national security documents, it fails to identify clearly this terror threat as originating from the Islamist ideology and those Muslims who evolve into that Islamist worldview. The NSCT acknowledges to the critical nature of the Internet including its role as a recruiting tool, but it fails to document the volume of Islamist ideology, strategy, and/or theory commonly accessed by vulnerable "seekers" who formulate the Islamist recruiting base. The NSCT does drive a "war of ideas" discussion and provides U.S. values guidance that can be useful in a greater strategic communications campaign.

The publication of a NSCT is value-added at the national level. As an unclassified document, it is light on detail and obviates politically incorrect facts, but its unclassified nature allows it to be widely accessed by global audiences. Although vague, the publication of an NSCT should drive the publication of subordinate CT strategies by the DoD, DoS, DHS, and other national security organizations, but it has not.[21]

---

the authority to detain) based on the Authorization for the Use of Military Force, Pub.L.107-40, 115 Stat.224 (2001).

[19] U.S. President, *NSCT,* 3.

[20] Ibid., 1.

[21] DoD and DoS have yet to publish authoritative strategies for counterterrorism. DHS has a strategy, but it is superficial. Under current foreign-versus-domestic restrictions, all three departments should have nested CT strategies which stress cooperation, but they do not. USSOCOM is the DoD lead

Executive Order 13584:  The Strategic Communications Initiative

In September of 2011, President Obama temporarily established the Center for Strategic Counterterrorism Communications (CSCC) within the DoS, tasking it to head interagency strategic communication efforts aimed at countering Islamist ideology and anti-U.S. messaging.[22]  The President established the organization in order to "support certain government-wide communications activities directed abroad."  Specifically, the order directs the new DoS component to:

> . . . coordinate, orient, and inform Government-wide public
> communications activities directed at audiences abroad and targeted against
> violent extremists and terrorist organizations, especially al-Qa'ida and its
> affiliates and adherents, with the goal of using communications tools to
> reduce radicalization by terrorists and extremist violence and terrorism that
> threaten the interests and national security of the United States.[23]

The CSCC was established under the Secretary of State with additional direction to establish an interagency advisory Executive Steering Committee to be chaired by the Under Secretary of State for Diplomacy and with membership including DoD and Office of the Joint Chiefs of Staff (JCS) representation.  On 26 March 2012, then-Secretary of State Clinton formally appointed Ambassador Albert Fernandez as the first CSCC Coordinator.[24]  Although the staffing of the Center is not specified, the document does authorize voluntary (unfunded) contributions from non-DoS organizations including

---

for CT, and yet USSOCOM also has failed to publish a CT strategy; perhaps because it is waiting for DoD leadership.  USSOCOM should drive this initiative by publishing the DoD-level guidance it would like to have under its own cover with the intent to assume the DoD lead and in the hope that DoD will functionally adopt the USSOCOM strategy in subsequent years.  Until then, any published DoD CT strategy would aid in the filling of the guidance void and would be most welcome by the CT community.

[22] U.S. President, *Executive Order 13584 – Developing an Integrated Strategic Counterterrorism Communications Initiative.* (Washington, DC:  Government Printing Office, 2001):  1-4.

[23] Ibid., 2

[24] U.S. Department of State, *Media Note – 26 March 2012,*  (PRN: 2012/456), Washinton, DC.

DoD. Further, the order directs DoS to coordinate CSCC activities with the National Counterterror Center. The CSCC's specified counterterror functions include:

- monitoring and evaluation of narratives and events;

- identifying current and emerging trends;

- developing and promulgating narratives and strategies;

- responding to and rebutting extremist messaging and narratives; and

- expanding, and coordinating the use of communications technologies.

Perhaps the most impactful portion of the document is this policy statement:

> Section 1. Policy. The United States is committed to actively countering the actions and ideologies of al-Qa'ida, its affiliates and adherents, other terrorist organizations, and violent extremists overseas that threaten the interests and national security of the United States. These efforts take many forms, but all contain a communications element and some use of communications strategies directed to audiences outside the United States to counter the ideology and activities of such organizations. These communications strategies focus not only on the violent actions and human costs of terrorism, but also on the narratives that can positively influence those who may be susceptible to radicalization and recruitment by terrorist organizations.[25]

The statement is particularly meaningful in this work because it clearly establishes a USG position that confronts not only destructive actions, but the ideologies of al-Qaeda and their ilk because they are a threat to U.S. interests and national security. The policy also acknowledges the Islamists' use of "communications strategies" in expanding their ideologies in both the radicalization process and the recruitment of potential terrorists.

Although the mission of this relatively new organization appears clearly aligned, real problems in execution remain. Other DoS Public Diplomacy strategy documents

---

[25] U.S. President, *Executive Order 13584*, 1-4.

seem to identify accurately the crucial nature of U.S. engagement in the war-of-words, but those words fail to translate into action. A DoS document 2012 document titled *Public Diplomacy: Strengthening U.S. Engagement with the World: A Strategic Approach for the 21st Century* highlights as Current Challenges that (1) violent extremists effectively use a wide variety of media platforms to inspire new followers and (2) the United States still has not developed an effective approach to countering their propaganda.[26] It lists disconnects between foreign policy formation and public diplomacy, shows a lack of mechanisms to link environmental assessments with plans and policies, and notes that there is structural weakness in strategic interagency communications.[27] In summary, the public diplomacy organization charged by the President with leading the U.S. fight in the war-of-ideas itself concludes that the U.S. effort remains ineffective and is a losing proposition.

Although this is the most specific of any Obama administration policy/strategy document, from a counterterror perspective it fails to identify clearly Islamists even once and does not mention in any form the words "Islam" or "Muslim." When the document does reference radicalization or radical ideologies, it references them within the context of "al-Qa'ida's ideology" and does not identify them as Muslim Islamist ideology. Frequently public statements and/or speeches by the President and other national leaders claim that al-Qaeda is all but defeated, which misleads casual listeners to assume that expending further effort to counter al-Qaeda is moot. Most importantly, such claims do not exist as statements of policy at the national level that causes greater disconnects. As

---

[26] U.S. Department of State, *Public Diplomacy: Strengthening U.S. Engagement with the World: A Strategic Approach for the 21st Century,* (November 2012): 14-15.

[27] Ibid., 17.

shown above, the NSS and subordinate national strategy documents fail to discuss publicly Islamic radicalization and the threats resulting from Islamist ideology in a way that would drive appropriate subordinate priorities and the allocation and prioritization of scarce national resources.

## The Department of State:  Quadrennial Diplomacy and Development Review

> Development, diplomacy, and defense, as the core pillars of American foreign policy, must mutually reinforce and complement one another in an integrated and comprehensive approach to national security.[28]
>
> – Quadrennial Diplomatic and Development Review, 2010

At the direction of Secretary Clinton, and borrowing from the DoD Quadrennial Defense Review (QDR) process, DoS published its first Quadrennial Diplomacy and Development Review (QDDR) under the title *Leading Through Civilian Power*.  The hefty 220-page document has received mostly negative reviews, due in part to its mass as well as its dearth of executable details.  However, review of the document for the purpose of this thesis in order to identify threads related to terror, Islamism, or radicalization was not fruitless.

The QDDR calls for creation of a new Bureau for Counterterrorism[29] and pledges to work with Congress to secure legislation and resources for that bureau by elevating the Office of the Coordinator for Counterterrorism to Bureau status.  This new office is not to be confused with, nor would it own, the new CSCC (introduced above) which would remain embedded in the DoS Public Diplomacy establishment.  This new office has as

---

[28] U.S. Department of State, *(QDDR) Leading Though Civilian Power: The First Quadrennial Diplomacy and Development Review*, (2010), 21.

[29] U.S. Department of State, *QDDR*, 45.

the dual goal of increasing the efficacy and visibility of DoS interagency counterterror efforts, as well as becoming the advocate for foreign diplomatic efforts advancing U.S. counterterror goals.  The QDDR includes a significant discussion of cyberspace and cyber threats,[30] but does not address the use of the Internet and/or mass media to distribute terrorist propaganda, terrorist strategy, nor advancing anti-U.S. Islamist ideology that opens the radicalization process to individuals and seeks recruitment of future terrorists.  After all, "public diplomacy seeks to help shift perceptions . . ."[31]

The QDDR's sub-chapter on Public Diplomacy repeats the standard terminologies and reminds the reader that its 2010 strategic framework was intended as a roadmap for aligning public diplomacy with foreign policy objectives.  Within the very short section (less than half a printed page) on Countering Violent Extremism, the QDDR presents U.S. public diplomacy themes with the statement that "Our responses must be both anticipatory and rapid, emphasizing a positive American narrative," and using accurate information to isolate and counter al-Qaeda's radicalized theme.  The QDDR briefly discusses the CSCC and it function to coordinate, orient, and inform whole-of-government communications activities targeting extremism to audiences abroad.[32]

Critique:  The QDDR is "hefty on pages and light on substantive content."[33] Public statements by DoS offices are consistent with President Obama's theme that al-Qaeda is virtually dead, the wars in the Middle East are over, and threats posed by radicalized Islamists are vastly overstated.[34]  Given the size of the document, its lack of

---

[30] Ibid., 45-49.

[31] Ibid., 60.

[32] Ibid., 45.

[33] U.S. Senate, 8-12..

[34] U.S. Department of State, *QDDR,* 143

terror content implies great effort was taken in its drafting to avoid the topic. This illustrates the degree of disconnect between previous Department of Defense (DoD) and Central Intelligence Agency (CIA) leadership statements about the critical and enduring nature of the Long War against the Global Islamist (Jihadist) Movement and the Obama administration's restrictive policy statements.

The Department of State: Strategic Plan for Fiscal Years 2007-2012

Late in the Bush administration's last term, then-Secretary of State Condoleezza Rice signed a revised version of the DoS Strategic Plan for the forthcoming presidential term. The contrast between that document and the later-issued QDDR is noteworthy in several regards. For instance, in her cover memo Secretary Rice highlighted key U.S. principles by saying:

> We must show the immorality and hollowness of the ideology of hatred that fuels violent extremism and, at the same time, foster development to combat poverty and to lay foundations for economic prosperity, human rights, and democracy.[35]

The 2007 Strategic Plan revision provided the following, formal mission statement:

> Mission Statement: Advance freedom for the benefit of the American people and the international community by helping to build and sustain a more democratic, secure and prosperous world composed of well-governed states that respond to the needs of their people, reduce widespread poverty, and act responsibly within the international system.[36]

The document outlined a framework of strategic goals. The discussion under Strategic Goal 1 (Achieving Peace and Security) included counterterrorism, conflict prevention, transnational crime, security cooperation, and homeland security matters.

---

[35] U.S. Deparment of State, *Strategic Plan: Fiscal Years 2007-2012*, (Revised May 7, 2007): 5.

[36] U.S. Departmentof State, *Strategic Plan 2007*, 17.

Under Strategic Goal 2 (Governing Justly and Democratically) the discussion included the rule of law, human rights, political competition, good governance, and building civil societies. Strategic Goal 6 included discussion of nurturing common interests, marginalizing extremists, and offering a positive vision of the United States, its intentions, and its citizens.[37]

Public Diplomacy: Promoting International Understanding:[38]

We will build trusted networks that undermine, marginalize, and isolate terrorists: discredit ideologies of hate and violence: and deliver legitimate alternatives to extremism.[39]

The document advocates that our values as a nation and as a people are the foundation of international engagement. They unapologetically define who we are as a people. This 2007, Bush-era document clarifies three strategic priorities to govern American public diplomacy: Positive Vision, Marginalize Extremism, and Nurture Common Interests and Values.

Offer a Positive Vision: The vision of the United States is deeply rooted in freedom of expression, freedom of religion, and human dignity. The DoS planned to advance this objective by transmitting a clear and compelling story advancing American values, clarifying untrue messaging, and advertising the good works of Americans (which are too often unrecognized). "Factual information is the antidote to ignorance, misunderstanding, and violent extremist."[40]

---

[37] Ibid., 10.

[38] Ibid., 34.

[39] Ibid., 12.

[40] U.S. Deparment of State, *Strategic Plan 2007*. 35.

Marginalize Extremism:  The document stressed the intent to isolate and undermine violent extremists who threaten the freedom and peace of all civilized peoples. It directs the DoS to discredit terror ideologies, delegitimize terror as an acceptable tactic to achieve political ends, and to end perceptions that the U.S. is hostile to any religion,[41] which implies Islam, but without saying so.  The strategy directed outreach to key interlocutors including religious leaders, youth, females, teachers, and journalists.  As a priority, the strategy would focus on truth-policing actions designed to counter perceived grievances, with the intent of interrupting the radicalization and recruitment processes. Media attention empowers terrorism as a strategy; therefore, journalists play a central role in the perceived grievance, misinformation, and radicalization process because they shape public opinion.  DoS directed an environment of openness would be designed to delegitimize terror by dialog and open debate, and by fostering grassroots condemnation of violence.

Strategic Communications:  The strategy specified, "all outreach efforts and communications should be infused with our values"[42] as part of a continued theme defining who we are as a people.  Later, the strategy takes note of DoD capabilities and tasks DoD to provide global support to public diplomacy as a principle player in the interagency process.[43]

The Near East:  The strategy acknowledged, "The Near East presents dangerous challenges to the United States . . ."[44] and continues into short discussions of key

---

[41] Ibid., 34-38.

[42] Ibid., 36.

[43] U.S. Deparment of State, *Strategic Plan 2007,* 37.

[44] Ibid., 50.

countries. Within discussions of Security Issues and Public Diplomacy, the document required working to eliminate disenfranchisement and despair, which contribute to the perception of grievance and aid the terrorist recruitment process. A key component of the U.S. strategic objective to provide support for political reform and the democratization process included effective public diplomacy in order to communicate U.S. policies assertively and to correct popular misconceptions about the United States, our values, or our intentions within that region.[45]

Critique: The 2007 document is far more detailed, linear, and openly advocates the U.S. position to target the source of the U.S.' terror problem. It formed a public roadmap that anyone seeking to understand U.S. values, U.S. strategy, and U.S. objectives could understand. It advocated for action against the psychological factors that create pro-terrorist environments, which creates the terrorists themselves, and it sought to foster their support. While this strategic plan also fails to use the term "Islamists," or forms of the word "Islam,' it does accurately satisfy the void noted in psychological and academic studies for use within a U.S. counterpropaganda campaign. Unfortunately, this 2007 Bush-era document was rejected by the Obama administration and replaced with the QDDR.

The Department of Defense: Quadrennial Defense Review

The most recent DoD Quadrennial Defense Review[46] (QDR) was signed by then-Secretary of Defense Gates and published in February 2010. At the time it was drafted and ultimately approved, the United States was fully committed to the wars in the Middle

---

[45] Ibid., 51.

[46] U.S. Department of Defense, *National Military Strategy* (Washington, DC: Government Printing Office, 2011): 1-34.

East; therefore, the document is considered a wartime QDR. As such, it attempted to balance the urgent and near-term requirements of winning those wars while allowing for long-term planning toward future threats. Like other DoD policy products,[47] the scope of the document focuses appropriately on the means to counter terrorism and less on the policies. However, the other DoD documents do highlight the interpretation of national strategic guidance at Department level. Further, they describe the means with which future combat against violent extremists, like the Islamists, will be conducted. The QDR lumps counterinsurgency (COIN), stability, and counterterror operations into a single group, within which it highlights initiatives to increase Special Operations Forces (SOF) capacity, increase COIN SOF-like capacity within the general purpose forces, and strengthen Strategic Communications capabilities. It highlights increased requirements for expertise in Languages, Regions, and Cultures across the force for increased activity in Security Cooperation, Foreign Internal Defense, and Security Assistance missions supporting partner nations. "Strategic Communications are essential in COIN, CT and Stability Operations . . . ."[48] Within Strategic Communications, the QDR calls for strengthening of key support capacities, noting the requirement to coordinate within the interagency Strategic Communications community and to coordinate policy implementation and information operations in support of national objectives.

---

[47] The Guidance for the Employment of the Force (or GEF) is a classified document and, therefore, cannot be assessed herein. Although there are summary notes of previous GEFs, the use of suspect summations is rejected.

[48] U.S. Department of Defense, *NMS,* 25.

The Secretary of Defense: Defense Strategic Guidance (2012)

In January 2012 the Secretary of Defense updated his guidance by way of a separate Defense Strategic Guidance (DSG) under the title *Sustaining U.S. Global Leadership: Priorities for 21st Century Defense.* The document's timing (two years into the four-year QDR cycle) was significant because it superseded elements of previous defense guidance. As an indicator of the political coordination and power of the document, it contains a White House cover letter signed by President Obama. One of Obama's noteworthy paragraphs consists of a statement that the review was driven by the nation's enduring national security interests and continues with reaffirmation that the U.S. seeks security, prosperity, and an international order wherein human rights are honored.

The document begins its assessment of the environment by recounting the damage inflicted on al-Qaeda and its leadership, and assesses the organization as "far less capable."[49] It continues by restating the global and enduring nature of al-Qaeda and its affiliates. A statement of policy, seemingly authored so that it can quoted, reads:

> For the foreseeable future, the United States will continue to take an active approach to countering these threats by monitoring the activities of non-state threats worldwide, working with allies and partners to establish control over ungoverned territories, and directly striking the most dangerous groups and individuals when necessary.[50]

---

[49] U.S. Department of Defense, *The Defense Strategic Guidance (DSG): Sustaining U.S. Global Leadership Priorities for the Twenty First Century.* (Washington, DC: Government Printing Office, January 2012): 1.

[50] Ibid., 3.

Of note, the document includes statements that the Arab Awakening[51] offers the United States "challenges," while it highlights regime changes, reform, and uncertainty as characteristics of the region's future. The DSG establishes the primary missions of the U.S. Armed Forces in order to achieve the objectives of the 2010 NSS. Noteworthy to this work, the first mission listed is Counter Terrorism and Irregular Warfare. The paragraph discusses the DoD working with other elements of national power to sustain pressure on al-Qaeda and its affiliates, and the need to expand counterterror and irregular warfare capabilities. Within the mission discussion for the defense of the homeland, the DSG only references defense from direct attack by non-state actors. The DSG does not discuss the radicalization process, motivational drivers that create terrorists, or the strategic communications/public diplomacy efforts outlined above.

### The Secretary of Defense: National Defense Strategy (2008)

> We face a global struggle. Like Communism and fascism before it, extremist ideology has transnational pretensions, and like its secular antecedents, it draws adherents from around the world.[52]
>
> – National Defense Strategy, 2008

In June of 2008, then-Secretary of Defense Robert Gates released his National Defense Strategy (NDS) to inform the defense enterprise of our national priorities. In striking contrast, this Bush-era document contains an entire section titled Win the Long

---

[51] A reference to the series of revolts which led to regime changes in many Muslim majority nations across the Middle East and Northern Africa. In those revolts, the Muslim Brotherhood and al-Qaeda fighters moved into these situations and are playing an important roles. The Muslim brotherhood took control of the Egyptian parliament and later the presidency. Since then, Egypt's policies have shifted sharply away from the West. In Libya, fighters apparently linked with al-Qaeda murdered the U.S. ambassador and three other Americans. Other governments may yet fall to these "popular revolts," but only time will tell if these are democratic movements or manifestations of the Islamist Movement. Early indicators imply the latter, not the former.

[52] U.S. Department of Defense, *NDS,* 7.

War and establishes the Long War as the "central objective of the U.S." for the foreseeable future. It describes the need as an extended series of campaigns to defeat violent extremist groups, presently led by al-Qaeda. It directs a U.S. effort to reduce support to extremists and encourage moderate voices, offering positive alternatives to the extremists' future vision. It predicts that fighting will be long-term, episodic, multi-front and multi-dimensional, an environment more complex and diverse than the Cold War. It specifies a war of idealist mindset that will require patience, creativity and patience. It notes the role of globalization, technology, and the Internet as adding to the spread and efficacy of the movement.

The NDS references COIN doctrinal terms in noting that the these campaigns are a violent struggle for legitimacy and influence over populations, and it stresses the need for the United States to understand and address the grievances that lie at the heart of these insurgencies. It concludes with the statement that "Victory will include discrediting extremist ideology, creating fissures between and among extremist groups and reducing them to the level of nuisance groups which can be tracked and handled by law enforcement capabilities."[53]

Critique: The distinction between the Bush-era NDS and the Obama-era document as it applies to clarity of purpose in the confrontation of violent extremists and the Global Islamist Movement is striking. In his NDS, Gates uses moralistic terms that reduce the conflict to its essence. Further, he informs the defense enterprise that this new Long War is an enduring threat that will require persistent effort, just as was required to win the Cold War, thereby framing the mindsets of national security planners.

---

[53] U.S. Department of Defense, *NDS,* 9.

# CHAPTER 7: CONCLUSIONS AND RECOMMENDATIONS

## A Summary

The previous chapters of this work have summarized the findings of psychological research proving that terrorists are not mentally ill, but rather that terrorists make rational decisions for reasons that are perfectly logical to them from their worldview. Those decisions are often incited to action by some key trigger or traumatic event, but are driven by perceived grievance, frustration, and a need to act in defense of the terrorists' ideals. This work summarized a literalist's interpretation of the Quran and its associated body of works, its historic narrative, and the traditions that continue to empower fundamentalist thought with glorious images of past conquests and imperial greatness. That history and evolved Quranic jurisprudence include control mechanisms which serve as useful tools to stifle reform, ostracize opposition, and silence counterbalancing voices of moderation. As a result, understanding the established concepts of precedence, innovation, deception, excommunication, and holy war is of primary importance to any would-be scholar attempting to contextualize the ongoing Global Islamist Movement that exploits these factors toward reestablishing and expanding a Muslim empire under Islamist Sharia law. This movement is not benign and actively seeks the destruction of the United States (U.S.) as a primary intermediate objective. U.S. policy should reflect that fact.

> Reversing this decline in U.S. strategic competence is an urgent issue for American national security in the twenty-first century.[54]

---

[54] Andrew Krepinevich and Barry Watts, "Regaining Strategic Competence," *Strategy for the Long Haul Series*, Center for Strategic and Budgetary Assessment (2009): http://www.csbaonline.org/4 Publications/PubLibrary/R.20090901.Regaining_Strategi/R.20090901.Regaining_Strategic.pd, (accessed February 15, 2013).

– Andrew Krepinevich

A letter from Senator Joe Lieberman to then-Deputy National Security Advisor John Brennan attests, "the term 'Islamist extremism' does not appear in two critical national security documents released by the Administration in 2010."[55] This is in part due to the Islamic Movement's campaign, but equally because the U.S. security strategists are caught in a modernist cultural appreciation of Islam as opposed to an objective critical assessment. Josef Pieper wrote, "we are faced, in short, with the threat that communication as such decays, that public discourse becomes detached from the notions of truth and reality."[56]

The preceding literature review of national security documents is not exhaustive. The nature of this work required that the literature review be constrained to national, unclassified documents. This is required not only so that this work remain within the unclassified domain, but also because of the interrelationship of U.S. messaging to the radicalization process. The nature of the problem resides within the unclassified domain; therefore, the solution resides there also.

In December 2011, the Senate Committee on Homeland Security and Governmental Affairs report on Islamist Radicalization concluded that Islamists formed a persistent, enduring, and dominant threat to the United States and its military.[57] Because of those findings, the Senate expressed its disapproval with the administration's strategy in three areas: (1) a failure to identify Islamist ideology as the root cause of terrorism; (2)

---

[55] Senator Joseph Lieberman, *Memo to the Honorable John Brennan* (April 9, 2010), http://def enddemocracy.org/images/stories/4_9_10_Final_Letter_to_Brennan_re_Islamist_extremism.pdf, (accessed February 15, 2013).

[56] Josef Pieper, *Abuse of Language, Abuse of Power,* (San Francisco,CA: Ignatius Press, 1988): 27

[57] U.S. Senate, *Committee Report,* Pg 10.

a failure to address the Internet's role in radicalization; and (3) a failure to go robustly after the threat.[58] The preceding literature review of U.S. national security policies confirms the Congressional assertions. As has been shown, the shift in wording and specificity between Bush-era and Obama-era strategy, as applied to terrorism, indicates that the Obama administration has carefully worded its guidance to avoid references that might offend but, in doing so, it has also removed authoritative guidance required for substantive subordinate strategies. It not only fails to specify that Islamist ideology is the cause of terrorism, but it also fails to mention "Islam" or 'Islamist" in the generic. The role of the Internet is acknowledged, but the organizations designed to represent U.S. interests are under-resourced and misaligned within the Department of State (DoS). As a result, Islamist dominance of the Internet remains virtually unchallenged. The Senate's final charge–"a failure to pursue the threat robustly"–requires both acknowledgement and action. Following a review of these national documents it is easy to conclude that there is no "robust U.S. strategy" to counter the Global Islamist Movement threat.

## Key Findings: A War of Ideas

Long-term stability, peace, and prosperity depend on the ongoing struggle within Islam itself, a war-of-ideas.[59] The rejection of the current and increasing wave of radicalization in favor of moderate forms of Islam requires an internal decision (that is, internal to the greater community of Muslims) to "modernize," which is counter to Islam's very nature and will not happen without some bloody internal reformation. This war of ideas will have violent aspects, but it will not be fought with tanks. Instead, this

---

[58] U.S. Senate, *Committee Report*, 2-4.

[59] Gabriel, 45-52.

war will be fought within the mass media outlets, particularly in social networking venues. Half-truths, propaganda, and centuries old suspicion complicate cross-cultural communications. Although globalization and the interconnected nature of modern media remain the radical's focal complaint of Western assaults against the world's Muslims, these same interactions are the best forum for increased moderation. This is unlikely to happen by way of the existing media outlets available throughout the Muslim world. They are, as a whole, either government-funded or are completely reliant on government influence for their survival; as a result, they are omni-ready to perform the government's bidding. Within the Muslim world, government media tends to portray the United States in a negative light and almost never acknowledges the "global force for good" that the United States often is. The United States serves as a scapegoat for their failed policies and their inability to adapt in today's world. As such, the United States serves as the uniting external enemy to distract the population from internal woes. The modern concept of an independent media responsible to the populace has not yet solidified in the region. As a result, "Radio Free America"-type broadcasts and the uncontrollable Internet can provide this critical capacity for the free exchange of information. More importantly, Western media, American media, and U.S. Government officials must start performing as "truth police" by holding Middle Eastern media outlets to account for their misinformation and exposing their manipulations in ways that publicly, and perhaps painfully, set the record straight.

## Public Diplomacy: The Problem

The post-9/11 goodwill that the United States enjoyed globally has vanished, but that did not happen because of any one event. It happened over time and from neglect.

To say that the United States lost the information war over-implies that the United States was even fighting information battles. It was not. A "glass is half full" apologist might explain the situation by naively stating that the United States did not feel a need to explain itself and that its actions would "speak for themselves," but reality proves that the United States has completely failed to persuade the Muslim world of its good intentions or the relative value of its objectives. Meanwhile, the writings of al-Suri, bin-Laden, and other Islamists continue to influence new generations of Muslims into the radicalization process, through militantism and into violent Jihadism,[60] and they do this throughout the information domain in a manner worthy of Madison Avenue.[61]

The various elements of the U.S. Government and its national security structures each have seemingly disconnected roles to play within this same strategic geo-political imperative: messaging. There are public diplomacy, public affairs, civil affairs, psychological operations, information operations, foreign policy, foreign affairs, and intelligence organizations[62] that influence the question. That is not to say that the United States has not made efforts toward public diplomacy. In 2007, the United States established the Counterterrorism Communications Center (CTCC) to provide interagency leadership and coordination in the war-of-ideas, and to integrate and improve the government's public diplomacy counterterror efforts, and positioned the CTCC within

---

[60] Richard Halloran. "Strategic Communications." *Parameters.* (Autumn, 2007): 4-14.

[61] The USAF's AFDD 2-5 Information Operations (11 Jan 2005) discusses Influence Operations (IOs) as the employment of capabilities to effect behaviors to achieve desired effects across the cognitive domain in order to change behavior and/or change the adversary's decision cycle. Doctrinally, IOs are designed to focus on affecting the perceptions and behaviors of leaders, grounds and entire populations. IOs effect behaviors, communicate intent, and change adversary decisions. Counter-propaganda is defined as activities which counter adversary propaganda and messaging to expose our adversary's attempts to influence target populations.

[62] Not an exhaustive list; this lexicon of apparent synonyms is part of the problem.

State's Bureau of International Information Programs.[63]  The nation's CTCC is simply

misaligned to the real task; therefore, it has failed.  Coordination for both consistent

theme and the content of the messaging is critical to consistency and effect.  The

intelligence community, in particular, must share and declassify information for use in

this war-of-ideas.[64]

## The Message:  To Represent U.S. Values, Intent, and Action

To fight and conquer in all your battles is not supreme excellence; supreme
excellence consists in breaking the enemy's resistance without fighting.
                                                                    – Sun Tzu[65]

In simple terms, strategic communications is a way of explaining one's ideas in an

effort to persuade (or neutralize) target populations toward understanding and accepting

one's policies and/or actions.  Strategic communications persuade friends to stand with

you and persuade neutrals to come over to your side or to just remain neutral.

Sending a successful message assumes that the message is based on a defensible

policy, a respectable identity, or a worthy core value.  The message must say precisely

and clearly what is meant.  Words are important, all the  more so when they target people

from different cultures, people whose first language is not English and people who will

translate that message for foreign retransmission; therefore, the message must be clear,

thought through thoroughly and tested for possible cultural and linguistic

misinterpretations.[66]  Within this context, shorter messages are better, but careful wording

and execution are required because the extremists which the messaging is attempting to

---

[63] Halloran, 4-14.

[64] Nacos, 22-25.

[65] Sun Tzu, 84.

[66] Halloran, 4-14.

delegitimize will interpret U.S. messaging as another attempt by "Western crusaders" to impose their foreign values upon the world's Muslims.[67]

The most difficult part of messaging is finding the means with which to transmit the message to the desired audience successfully; in this case, with the goal of dissuading potential Islamic insurgents globally.[68] The magnitude of the task dictates the use of every possible channel of communications as frequently as possible. Messaging which is transmitted by national leadership personally is the most valuable, particularly in times of crisis when their words are most likely to be replayed globally. Key statements and phrases woven consistently into other speeches are most impactful. Given the media's tendency to edit comments into succinct sound bites, the essence of these messages must be condensed to provide that sound bite correctly.

## The Truth: Be the Truth Police

> Never allow the enemy's misinformation to go stand unchallenged and
> never lie. All warfare is based on deception.
> 
> – Sun Tzu[69]

Everything within the realm of strategic communications should be as truthful as possible, even when it hurts and even when classification restrictions will not allow the entire truth to be shared. Any perceived manipulation of facts and misinformation will be discovered and will be used as a blunt instrument against the United States.[70]

---

[67] Nacos, 26-28.

[68] Because the mechanisms for recruiting, radicalization, and transition to violence are the same for all Jihadists, and because the battle of ideas is universally fought on the Internet, this strategy would have an equal impact on domestic (U.S., homegrown) and foreign terrorism.

[69] Sun Tzu, 84.

[70] Nacos, 26-30.

Political Correctness:  The Battle for the Internet

The Internet is this century's strategic communications battlefield, and U.S. over-sensitivity toward "manipulation" and free speech has resulted in the functional concession of the Internet to the Jihadists.  The *Economist* magazine, published in England, has conducted solid reporting on the Muslim infiltration of the Internet for Jihad.  It concluded, "the Internet gives Jihadists an ideal vehicle for propaganda, provides access to large audiences free of government censorship or media filters, while carefully preserving their anonymity."  Further, the *Economist* highlighted the fact that the Internet allows Jihadists the opportunity to connect disparate Jihadist individuals and groups to create a sense of a global Jihadi movement and membership within a greater Jihadi community and that are all inspired to defend the global Muslim community from its common cultural enemy.  They continued by noting the ease and low costs associated with the use of the Internet and the exponential impact of Jihadi propaganda by attaching sound, video, and pictures to those web sites.  "In short, the hand-held video camera has become as important a tool of insurgency as the AK-47 or the RPG rocket launchers."[71]

Warning:  A Conflict in Strategic Objectives

As the U.S. Government acknowledges the threat posed by this global Islamist insurgency, socializes awareness of "this new Cold War" and then mobilizes a national effort (with popular support) for action against that threat, the United States must also acknowledge that these efforts risk granting de facto legitimacy to the very Islamic insurgents it seeks to delegitimize.  As with all counterinsurgency operations, the essence of this counter-Islamist struggle is for moderate legitimacy within the hearts and minds of

---

[71] "A World Wide Web of Terror," *The Economist*, (14 July 2007):  28-30.

the population. Within this counterinsurgency, the population is not confined within a specific geographic location. This population is dispersed globally and includes Muslims within the United States and its armed forces.

## Commit to Win:  The War of Ideas

The United States must get into the strategic communications[72] game as an essential element of national security toward winning the Long War. Strategic national leadership must recognize that this new Long War against the Global Islamist Movement equates to a global counterinsurgency; therefore, the same levels of sustained effort are required as were employed to contain the Soviets during the Cold War. The Islamists' own grand strategy clearly and repeatedly states that their information warfare effort is at least fifty percent of their strategic effort and that actual fighting is only a near-term tactic within their greater long-term strategy to gain the hearts and minds of the populace; yet they remain functionally unopposed by the United States in that domain. Thus far, U.S. efforts have been half-hearted at best and are best characterized as disconnected bureaucratic Band-Aids placed on a lethal wound. Revolutionary, not evolutionary, change is now required. The United States should immediately establish within the White House an Office of Strategic Communications with full Cabinet-level rank. This Director must attend all Cabinet and National Security Council meetings so that he can monitor events, provide advice on foreign perceptions of U.S. actions, and then both guide and coordinate U.S. messaging throughout the whole-of-government. The

---

[72] Influence Operations are designed to focus on affecting the perceptions and behaviors of leaders, grounds and entire populations. They are targeted to effect behaviors, communicate intent, and change adversary decisions. Counterpropaganda remains a central element of messaging, and prioritizes opposition to adversary propaganda and messaging in order to expose the adversary's attempts to influence the same target populations.

Director's primary responsibilities would be to apply factual messaging to counter the Islamist's recruiting strategies and specifically to counter their use of the Internet with all of the implements of U.S. national power.[73] The White House Office of Strategic Communications and its Director must remain apolitical; otherwise, it cannot truly serve the nation, but will degrade into a short-term propaganda ministry for the political party in power at the moment.[74] Without a long-term, Cold War-like vision of this new Long War, the effort will be pointless.

## Conclusions

The 9/11 surprise attacks against the United States shocked Americans and finally focused public attention toward the issue of modern Islamist terrorism. America oriented its wrath toward the destruction of al-Qaeda and, indeed, today al-Qaeda is significantly attrited, but it is far from dead. Even if it were, terrorism is but one asymmetric tactic and al-Qaeda is but one operational unit within a greater Global Islamist Movement. In 2001, America might have started fighting back, but its Global War on Terror was, by definition, a global war against a tactic and not against the strategic source of that tactic: the Islamists. Unilateral declarations of victory and military retractions from the Middle East will not make them go away. Even if ignored, they will not ignore the United States.

The Global Islamist Movement is not new. The movement has been formalizing its ideology and publishing its strategy since 1960s. They defeated the Soviet Union in Afghanistan and, afterwards, shifted their attention to the last remaining Western

---

[73] Specifically, U.S. diplomatic, information, military, and economic power must work in close coordination toward defined objectives. The concept highlights the need for whole-of-government effort and further implies that the Department of Defense might have only a supporting role in many actions.

[74] Halloran, 4-14.

superpower, the United States, as their primary target. Significantly aided by globalization, the Internet, and social media, the movement continues to gain momentum. It overtly seeks the destruction of the United States as the decisive point within its strategy for the general destruction of modern Western democratic ideology.

U.S. policy makers are traditionally hesitant to engage in governmental discussions that hint toward the free exercise of religion or which might appear to target other non-Anglo-Caucasian cultures because of proven fears of being branded as a racist, bigot, or both.[75] Public study and debate of these topics might be uncomfortable, but the fearful suppression of the dialog forms a U.S. strategic vulnerability. The United States must formally recognize that the Global Islamist Movement forms an enduring threat to U.S. domestic security and to U.S. national interests globally.

Today's Long War continues to be waged between the Islamists' seventh-century feudal ideology and a twenty-first century ideology of Western liberal democracy; the two are incompatible. They cannot currently coexist because the values of the one violate the values of the other, and the United States should not compromise its values as established within its Constitution and Declaration of Independence. Islamist ideology has evolved very little in the 1,381 years since Mohammad died because it rejects modernization as ungodly and idealizes the ancient past of a feudal society. Upon rare occasion, Muslim reformers have been able to progress the culture toward modernity only to have fundamentalists pull their society backward, back toward Mohammad's seventh-century. This conversation is correctly left to Muslims themselves, and luminary

---

[75] Steven Emerson, "Combating Lawfare," *IPT News*, (March 15. 2010), http://www.investigate project.org/1858/combating-lawfare, (accessed February 15, 2013).

authors like Youssef Aboul-Enein play an important role in moderation and the interception of would-be radicals.

"Remember, when you look at Islamic culture: it IS because it WAS."[76]

Recommendations

- Islamism is a political identity that accurately identifies the opposition; do not fear the term, but use it correctly.

- Islamist ideology is known and, therefore, is vulnerable.

- The United States must recognize that it is in a war (a "Long War") and assume a Cold War-like attitude toward winning that war. The term Long War should be adopted within the National Security Strategy and subordinate strategy documents in order to communicate the concept clearly and universally.

- Defending against the tactic of terrorism can never win the war. The U.S. effort must be placed toward "winning hearts and minds" campaigns, which are primarily fought over Internet.

- The Internet respects no national boundaries; therefore, U.S. policies, strategies, and laws must adapt to this new borderless paradigm.

- Clear, consistent, and carefully constructed statements of U.S. national vision, values, policy, and strategy not only accurately drive subordinate strategies and resources toward fighting this Long War effectively, but they also provide ideal data-points for the U.S. public diplomacy campaigns.

- There must be a common, consistent, enduring, party-neutral, and apolitical pro-U.S. messaging campaign. The organizational culture of the Department of State

---

[76] Gabriel, 44.

makes it incapable of leading the effort and, for a variety of reasons, the Department of Defense, the Department of Homeland Security, the Central Intelligence Agency, and other candidates are equally ill-suited for this function; therefore, a new Cabinet-level position is required for success.

- Win the Internet through aggressive messaging and truth policing.

- Win the war of ideas by advocating for U.S. core values.

- Recognize that political correctness endangers national security.

The United States should proudly advance its national interests and overtly advocate for the principles enshrined within its grand strategy: the Declaration of Independence and the U.S. Constitution. Western liberal democratic tradition is in direct opposition to the expanding ideology of the Global Islamist Movement. Fortunately, the Muslim masses do not yet agree with their Islamist ideology. To keep it that way, U.S. messaging must get better–and fast.

# BIBLIOGRAPHY

"A World Wide Web of Terror." *The Economist* (14 July 2007): 28-30.

Abizaid, John. "The Long War." *Harvard University, John F. Kennedy School of Government – Institute of Politics* (2006).

Aboul-Enein, Youssef. "Arab Strategic Thought: Egyptian Author Dr. Saleh Salem." *International Affairs: The FAO Journal* XIV, no. 3 (August 2011): 23-29.

Ali, Abdullah Yusuf (trans.). *The Holy Quran: Text, Translation, and Commentary.* Damascus, Syria: Arab Press and Distribution Company, 1987.

    *The Meaning of The Holy Qur'an: New Edition with Revised Translation, Commentary and the Newly Complied Comprehensive Index.* Beltsville, MA: Amana Publications, 2006.

Ali, Abdullah Yusuf and Mohammad Shirazi (trans.). *The Holy Quran.* Pakistan: Arab Press and Distribution Company, 1964.

Ali, Hashim Amir. *The Message of the Quran Presented in Perspective.* Vermont: Charles E. Tuttle Publishing Company, 1974.

Al-Misri, Ahmad ibn Naqib. *Reliance of the Traveler: A Classic Manual of Islamic Sacred Law.* Translated by Nug Ha Min Keller. Beltville, MD: Amana Publications, 1994.

Amini, Mohammad. *Fundamentals of Ijtehad.* Delhi, India: Aligarh Muslim University, 1986.

Avella, Valerie. "The Domestic War on Terror: Fighting the Roots of Jihadist Extremism in the U.S." *Defense Intelligence Journal* 15, no. 1 (2006): 13-24.

Baalkaki, Rohi. *Al-Mawrid: A Modern Arabic English Dictionary.* Beirut, Lebanon: Dar El-Elm Lil-Mayuayen, 1993.

Bennett, Brian. *Understanding, Assessing, and Responding to Terrorism: Protecting Critical Infrastructure and Personnel.* New Jersey: John Wiley & Sons Publishing, Inc., 2007.

Bergen, Peter. *Holy War, Inc.: Inside the Secret World of Osama Bin Laden.* New York, NY: The Free Press, 2001.

Bergen, Peter, and Brian Hoffman. *Assessing the Terrorist Threat: A Report of the Bipartisan Policy Center's National Security Preparedness Group.* Washington, DC: Bipartisan Policy Center, 2010.

Beaumont, Peter and Patrick Kingsley. "Violent Tide of Salafism Threatens the Arab Spring." *The Guardian.* February 9, 2013. http://www.guardian.co.uk/world /2013/feb/09/violent-salafists-threaten-arab-spring-democracies (accessed February 15, 2013).

Beutel, Alehandrao. *Radicalization and Homegrown Terrorism in Western Muslim Communities: Lessons Learned for America.* Washington, DC: Minaret of Freedom Institute, 2007.

Bongar, Bruce, Lisa Brown, Larry Beutler, and James Breckenridge (eds.). *Psychology of Terrorism.* Oxford, NY: Oxford University Press, 2007.

Borum, Randy. *Psychology of Terrorism.* Tampa, FL: University of South Florida, 2004.

Brachman, Jarret, and Alix Lavine. "You Too Can Be Awlaki!" *The Fletcher Forum of World Affairs Journal* 35, no. 25 (Winter, 2011). 25-46.

Brachman, Jarret and William McCants. *Stealing Al-Qaida's Playbook.* West Point, NY: Combating Terrorism Center, 2006.

Chalk, Peter, Angel Rabasa, William Rosenau, and Leone Piggott. *The Evolving Terrorist Treat to Southeast Asia: A Net Assessment.* Santa Monica, CA: National Defense Research Institute, 2009.

Cowan, Milton (trans.). *Hans Wehr: A Dictionary of Modern Standard Written Arabic.* Ithaca, NY: Spoken Language Services, Inc., 1993.

Daniel, Wallace. "Islam and the Clash of Civilizations." *Journal of Church and State* 48, no. 3 (Summer, 2006): 138-158.

Davis, Jacquelyn. *Radical Islamist Ideologies and the Long-War: Implications for US Strategic Planning and U.S. Central Command's Operations.* Washington, DC: Institute for Foreign Policy Analysis, Inc., 2007.

Dawood, N. J. (trans.). *The Koran.* New York, NY: Penguin Books, 1997.

Doniach, N., Safa Khulusi, N Shamaa, and W. Davin (eds.). *The Concise Oxford English-Arabic Dictionary of Current Usage.* Oxford, NY: Oxford University Press, 1982.

Dreazen, Yazi. "Muslim Population in the Military Raises difficult Issues." *The Wall Street Journal* (2009), http://online.wsj.com/article/SB125755 853525 335343.html. (accessed February 15, 2013).

Emerson, Steven. "Combating Lawfare." *IPT News.* (March 15, 2010), http://www.investigate project.org/1858/combating-lawfare, (accessed February 15, 2013).

Gabriel, Mark. *Culture Clash: Islam's War on the West.* Lake Mary, FL: Front Line Publishing: A Strang Company, 2007.

Gregg, Heather. "Fighting the Jihad of the Pen: Countering Revolutionary Islamic Ideology." *Terrorism and Political Violence* 22, no. 2 (2010): 292-314.

Halloran, Richard. "Strategic Communications." *Parameters* 37 (Autumn, 2007): 4-14.

Hargus, Coyt. "Ali and the Roots of Division within Islam." *International Affairs: The FAO Journal* XIV, no. 1 (February 2011): 20-24.

"Quranic Interpretation: True Messages vs. Manipulation." *International Affairs: The FAO Journal* XIV, no. 2 (May 2011): 20-23.

Hitchens, Christopher. *Jefferson's Quran: What the Founder Really Thought About Islam.* January 9, 2007. http://www.slate.com/articles/news_and_politics/ fightingwords/2007/01 /jeffersons_quran.html (accessed February 15, 2013).

Hoffman, Bruce. "The Leaderless Jihad's Leader: Why Osama Bin Laden Mattered." *Foreign Affairs Journal.* (May 13, 2011).

Howard, Michael. "A Long War?" *Survival.* 48, no. 4 (2006): 7-14.

Hudson, Rex. *The Sociology and Psychology of Terrorism: Who Becomes a Terrorist and Why?* Washington, DC: Research Division, Library of Congress, 2005.

Huq, Aziz. 'The Signaling Function of Religious Speech in Domestic Counter-Terrorism." *Texas Law Review* 89, no. 833: 834-900.

Ibrahim, Raymond. "Studying the Islamic Way of War: To know an enemy one must first acknowledge his existence." *The National Review.* (Sept 11, 2008) http://article. nationalreview.com/print/?q=NmE1ZTRmMDQxMDQ0ZmVmNWVkOTk5Mm M5YTQ4NmFhZjg. (accessed February 15, 2013)

Islamic City. *Tafsir.* http://islam.org /mosque/tafsir.htm (accessed October 15, 2012).

*The Holy Quran.* http://islam.org/mosque/Quran.htm (accessed October 15, 2012).

Israeli, Ralph. "A Manual of Islamic Fundamentalist Terrorism." *Terrorism and Political Violence* 14, no. 4: 23-40.

Jenkins, Brian. *Going Jihad: The Fort Hood Slayings and Home-Grown Terrorism.* Santa Monica, CA: RAND Corporation, 2009.

Jihad Watch. *Muslim Brotherhood – ISNA Convention: "Don't Talk to the FBI."* http://www.jihadwatch.org/cgi-sys/cgiwrap/br0nc0s/managed-mt/mt-search.cgi?

search=cair+islamis t+objectives&IncludeBlogs=1&limit=20. (accessed February 15, 2013).

*Rep. King Demands Answers about non-Prosecution of Hamas Linked CAIR: CAIR's Hoomer Complains.* http://www.jihadwatch.org/cgisys/cgiwrap/br0nc0s/managed-mt/mt-search.cgi?search=unindicted+coconspirators&IncludeBlogs=1&limit =20, (accessed February 15, 2013).

*The Victimology Subterfuge.* http://www.jihadwatch.org/cgi-sys/cgiwrap/br0nc0s/managed-mt/mt-search.cgi?search=Jihad+of+the+courts&IncludeBlogs=1&limit=20, (accessed February 15, 2013).

Kepel, Gilles. *Jihad: The Trials of Political Islam.* Translated by Anthony Roberts. London, UK: Tauris & Co. Ltd., 2003.

Kayani, Saima. "Islam: Past, Present, and Future." *The Dialogue* 6, no. 4 (2009): 320-338.

Khadduri, Majid. *War and Peace in the Law of Islam.* Baltimore, MD: Clark, NJ: Law Book Exchange, 2006.

Khalil, Lyndia. "U.S. Counter-Radicalization Strategy: The Ideological Challenge." *The Australian Strategic Policy Institute* 96 (January 11, 2012): 1-7.

Khan, Mehar Omar. "Is there an Islamic Way of War?" *The Small Wars Journal* 3 (2010): http://small warsjournal.com/blog/2010/03/is-there-an-islamic-way-of-war/, (accessed February 15, 2013).

Krepinevich, Andrew, and Barry Watts. "Regaining Strategic Competence." Strategy for the Long-Haul Series. Center for Strategic and Budgetary Assessments (2009), http://www. csbaonline.org/4Publications/PubLibrary/R.20090901.Regaining_Strategi/R.20090901.Regaining_Strategic.pdf, (accessed February 15, 2013).

Lacey, Jim. *A Terrorist's Call to Global Jihad: Deciphering Abu Musab Al-Suri's Islamic Jihad Manifesto.* Annapolis, MD: Naval Institute Press, 2008.

*The Cannons of Jihad: Terrorist's Strategy for Defeating America.* Annapolis, MD: Naval Institute Press, 2008.

Lewis, Bernard. *The Crisis of Islam: Holy War and Unholy Terror.* New York, NY: The Modern Library, 2003.

Liberman, Joseph (Senator). Memo to the Honorable John Brennan (April 9, 2010), http://def

enddemocracy.org/images/stories/4_9_10_Final_Letter_to_Brennan_re_Islamist_extremism.pdf, (accessed February 15, 2013).

Lizardo, Omar and Albert Bergesen. "Types of Terrorism by World System Location." *Humboldt Journal of Social Relations* 2, no. 27 (2008): 167-192.

Mainuddin, Rolin. "Political Islam: Untangling the Conceptual Muddle." *Journal of Third World Studies* 24, no. 2 (Fall, 2007): 109-128.

Malik, Salim. *The Quranic Concept of War.* New Delhi, India: Himalayan Books, 1986.

Melshen, Paul. "Mapping Out a Counter-Insurgency Campaign Plan: Critical Considerations in Counterinsurgency Campaigning." *Small Wars and Insurgencies* 18, no. 4, (December 2007): 665-698.

Nacos, Briqitte. *Terrorism and Counter-terrorism.* New York, NY: Longman-Pearson Education, Inc., 2011.

Naeman, Dorit. "Brides of Palestine/Angles of Death: Media, Gender, and Performance in a Case of the Palestinian Female Suicide Bomber." *SIGNS* 32, no. 4 (Summer, 2007): 930-943.

Naji, Abu Bakr. *The Management of Savagery: The Most Critical Stage Through Which the Umma Will Pass.* Translated by William McCants. Oxford, NY: Oxford University Press, 2011.

Ness, Cindy. "In the Name of the Cause: Women's Work in Secular and Religious Terrorism." *Studies in Conflict and Terrorism* 28 (2005): 353-373.

Neal, Mark. "Number of Muslims Living in the U.S. Doubles Since 9/11." *The Daily News.* http://www.nydailynews.com/news/national/number-muslims-u-s-doubles-9-11-article-1.1071895. (accessed February 15, 2013).

Pew Research. *Muslim Americans: Middle Class and Mostly Mainstream.* (2011) http://www.pew research.org /2007/05/22/muslim-americans-middle-class-and-mostly-mainstream/ (accessed February 15, 2013).

Pieper, Josef. *Abuse of Language, Abuse of Power.* San Francisco, CA: Ignatius Press, 1988.

Post, Jerrold. "When Hatred is Bred in the Bone: Psycho-cultural Foundations of Contemporary Terrorism." *Political Psychology* 26, no. 4 (August 2005): 615-636.

Sageman, Marc. *Leaderless Jihad: Understanding Terrorist Networks in the Twenty-First Century.* Philadelphia, PA: University of Pennsylvania Press, 2008.

*Understanding Terrorist Networks.* Philadelphia, PA: University of Pennsylvania Press, 2004.

Satloff, Robert. "Middle East Policy Planning for a Second Obama Administration." *Policy Watch* 1995 (November 9, 2012).

Savage, Charlie. "Secret U.S. Memo Made Legal Case to Kill a Citizen." *The New York Times.* October 8, 2011. http://www.uta.edu/ faculty/story/2311/Misc/2011,10,8, SecretUSMemoMadeLegalCaseToKillUSCitizen.pdf (accessed February 15, 2013).

Scheuer, Michael. *Through Our Enemies' Eyes. Osama bin Laden, Radical Islam, and the Future of America (Revised).* Dulles, VA: Potomac Books, Inc., 2006.

Shane, Scott, and Souad Mekhennet. "Imam's path from condemning terror to preaching Jihad." *The New York Times.* May 8, 2010. http://www.nytimes.com/2010/05/ 09/world/09awlaki.html ?ref=anwaralawlaki&_r=0 (accessed February 15, 2013).

Silber, Mitchell and Arvin Bhatt. *Radicalization in the West: The Homegrown Threat.* New York, NY: New York Police Department Intelligence Unit, 2007.

Silinsky, Mark. "Beyond Diversity and Tolerance: Reassessing Islam and Islamism in the U.S. Military." *International Affairs: The FAO Journal* 13, no. 2 (May 2010): 8-14.

Spencer, Robert. *The Politically Incorrect Guide to Islam (and the Crusades).* Washington, DC: Regency Publishing, Inc., 2005.

Staub, Ervin. "The Roots of Evil: The role of social conditions, culture, personality, systems of relations, and the destructive fulfillment of human needs in individual and group violence." *Personality and Social Psychology Review* 3, no. 3 (August 1999): 179-192.

Stout, Chris (ed.). *The Psychology of Terrorism: Theoretical Understandings and Perspectives (Vol. 3).* Westport, CT: Praeger Publishing, 2002.

Stout, Mark, Jessica Huckabey, and John Schindler with Jim Lacey. *The Terrorist Perspectives Project: Strategic and Operational Views of Al-Qaida and Associated Movements.* Annapolis, MD: Naval Institute Press, 2008.

Thayer, Bradley and Valerie Hudson. "Sex and the Shaheed: Insights from the Life Sciences on Islamic Suicide Terrorism." *International Security* 34, no. 4 (May 2011): 37-42.

Tzu, Sun. *The Art of War.* Translated by Samuel Griffith. London, UK: Oxford University Press, 1963.

U.S. Army and U.S. Marine Corps. *Counterinsurgency Field Manual.* Chicago, IL: University of Chicago Press, 2007.

U.S. Defense Intelligence Agency. *Sheikh Abdullah Azzam: Al-Qaida Al-Sulba The founding Father of Al-Qaida.* Norfolk, VA: U.S. Navy, Visual Information Directorate, 2008.

    *Abu Musab Al-Suri. The Clausewitz of Al-Qaida Ideology. 21st Century Al-Qaida Strategist.* Norfolk, VA: U.S. Navy, Visual Information Directorate, 2009.

U.S. Department of Defense. *Defense Strategic Guidance. Sustaining U.S. Global Leadership: Priorities for 21st Century Defense.* Washington, DC: Government Printing Office, January 2012.

    *National Military Strategy.* Washington, DC: Government Printing Office, 2011.

    *Quadrennial Defense Review.* Washington, DC: Government Printing Office, February 2010.

    "Field Manual 27-10. The Laws of Land Warfare." http://ac-support.europe. umuc.edu/~nstanton/FM27-10.htm (accessed September 4, 2012).

U.S. Department of Homeland Security. *Quadrennial Homeland Security Review Report: A Strategic Framework for a Secure Homeland.* Washington, DC: Government Printing Office, February 2010.

U.S. Department of State. *Strategic Plan: Fiscal Years 2007-2012.* Washington, DC: Government Printing Office, May 7, 2007.

    *Public Diplomacy: Strengthening U.S. Engagement with the World: A Strategic Approach for the Twenty First Century.* (November , 2012): 1-34.

    *Quadrennial Diplomatic Development Review: Leading Through Civilian Power.* Washington, DC: Government Printing Office, 2010.

    "Terrorist Exclusion List." http://www.state.gov/j/ct/ rls/other/des/123086.htm (assessed December 15, 2012).

U.S. House of Representatives Intelligence Committee. *Al-Qaeda: The Many Faces of an Islamist Extremist Threat.* Report to the House Permanent Select Committee on Intelligence. Washington, DC: Government Printing Office, June 2006.

U.S. Immigration and Naturalization Service. "List of terror organizations whose members and supporters are barred admission under the INA: The truth About the Pitts Legislation to Protect Vulnerable Refugees." http://www.rcusa.org/ uploads/pdfs/ms-legis-tiersgrps8-9-06.pdf (accessed February 15, 2013).

U.S. Marine Corps. *Small Wars Manual.* Washington, DC: Government Printing Office, 1940.

U.S. President. Executive Order #13224: "Blocking Property and Prohibiting Transitions With Persons Who Commit, Threaten to Commit, or Support Terrorism." Washington, DC: Government Printing Office. September 23, 2001.

*National Security Strategy.* Washington, DC: Government Printing Office, May 2010.

*National Security Strategy for Counterterrorism.* Washington, DC: Government Printing Office, June 28, 2011.

U.S. Senate. Homeland Security and Governmental Affairs Committee Report, *Violent Islamists Extremism, the Internet and Homegrown Terrorist Threat.* May, 2008.

Watts, Clint. *Major Nidal Hasan and the Fort Hood Tragedy: Implications for the U.S. Armed Forces.* (June, 2011): 1-7.

Yilmaz, Muzaffer. *Political Islam in the Context of Social Identity: The Effects of Perceived External Threats on the Rising Islamic Challenge.* Washington, DC: George Mason University Publications, 2002.

Zaidi, Syed. "The Fundamentalist Distortion of the Islamic Message." *Athena Intelligence Journal* 3, no. 4 (October-December, 2008): 59-75.

www.ingramcontent.com/pod-product-compliance
Lightning Source LLC
Chambersburg PA
CBHW081327310526
45789CB00018B/2455